The Hidden Spiritual Laws

"Why some people stay in failure and others break through to victory."

Copyright © 2023 by Don Kremer

All rights reserved solely by the author. The author guarantees all contents are original and do not infringe upon the legal rights of any other person or work. No part of this book may be reproduced in any form without the permission of the author. The views expressed in this book are not necessarily those of the publisher. Unless otherwise indicated, "Scripture taken from the NEW AMERICAN STANDARD BIBLE®
Copyright ©1960,1962,1963,1968,1971,1972,1973,1975,1977,1995 by The Lockman Foundation. Used by permission."

Special Thanks to Christina Holslaw for her editing of this book.

Dedication

To Jane, my wife.
A gift from the Lord to my life.

Table of Contents

Forward by David Michael ∗ 1

Introduction ∗ 3
The Sword

Chapter One ∗ 7
The Spiritual Law of Creative Design

Chapter Two ∗ 19
The Spiritual Law of Governing Authorities.

Chapter Three ∗ 33
The Spiritual Law of Sowing and Reaping

Chapter Four ∗ 44
The Spiritual Laws of Mercy, Grace, and the Government of Sin

Chapter Five ∗ 64
Removing the Sword

Chapter Six ∗ 82
The Spiritual Laws

Chapter Seven ∗ 90
The Spiritual Laws of Communication, Agreement Alignment, Confession, and Transfer

Chapter Eight ∗ 130
The Spiritual Law of Confession and the Law of Dignitary Authority

Chapter Nine ∗ 146
The Spiritual Laws of Separation and the Law of the Canopy

Chapter Ten ∗ 177
The Spiritual Law of Pairing

Chapter Eleven ∗ 195
The Spiritual Law of Forgiveness

Chapter Twelve ∗ 202
The Spiritual Law of Advancement

Chapter Thirteen ∗ 212
God's 100% Commitment to You

Forward

Forward
David J. Michael
Contributing author of the Spirit-Filled Bible, 1991 edition.

In more than twenty-five years that I have known and worked closely with Don Kremer, I have seen in him a living example of a devoted Christian life. His devotion to his Savior first of all is a shining light for other ministers to follow. His dedication to his three children, now adults, is exemplary. And his patient, devoted service to the congregations he has pastored truly sets him apart in today's world.

I have ministered with Pastor Don in three states and in one nation in the Former Soviet Union. Furthermore, Pastor Don has traveled with my Dad, Evangelist Dick Mills, and also frequently had my Dad minister as guest speaker in his congregation in Idaho. On one occasion, my Dad and I and Pastor Don travelled together to a small town in the western part of Wyoming, where Dad ministered. I can attest to the fact that my Dad always held Pastor Don in high regard. Don is the only person I know whom Dad featured in his own ministry newsletter as a guest writer. Considering the number of ministries who sought out Dad's endorsement, Pastor Don's sole inclusion speaks volumes.

Don Kremer and his wife Jane took me into their home on numerous occasions, the first of which comprised a period of two-and-a-half months in the summer of 2016, during which time Cheyenne became my home base for ministry in southeast Wyoming as well as on the Wind River Indian reservation in the central part of the state. Living in their home that summer, and in subsequent trips to Cheyenne in 2019 and 2021, gave me the opportunity to know that Don's godly

Forward

character is absolutely the same in private as it is in public ministry. He is real, and is a man of principle day in and day out.

Don's passion for the unreached people groups has driven him to go to Ghana in west Africa more than seventy-seven times—and always at his own expense. I cannot think of another minister with such a true record of service. His generosity is legendary, and his compassion for people ensnared in, and troubled by, life's bondages cannot be overstated.

Most significantly, I am confident in saying that Pastor Don Kremer takes his duty seriously to handle Scripture diligently and accurately, and in so doing to feed the Lord's people with godly knowledge as they are being guided into the Wisdom which is from Above. In my experience, Don Kremer is a living illustration of what being "a man of God" is all about. Would to God there were more like him.

David J. Michael
Contributing Author, Spirit-Filled Life Bible (Word Wealth, Old Testament) 1991 edition.
Hemet, California

INTRODUCTION

The Sword!

The word *"sword"* is used over four hundred times in the Old Testament and thirty-two times in the New Testament.

Ezekiel's prophecies against Israel mention the sword over eighty times. It is mostly used in two applications: (1) in the context of war and (2) as a metaphorical instrument of God's judgment. Sometimes it is a consequence such as captivity; sometimes it is famine. At other times, it is disease, troubles, or different types of plagues.

In the New Testament (Hebrews 4:13), God's Word is described as a two-edged sword that comes from the mouth of Christ (Revelation 1:16 and 2:12). In Romans 13:4, it is a metaphorical instrument of punishment for violating God's spiritual laws.

Throughout this book, the word *sword* is used to define the consequence or penalty for violating God's spiritual laws. It cuts according to the violation—whatever that might be. Galatians 6:7 warns us:

> *"Do not be deceived, God is not mocked* [He will not allow Himself to be ridiculed, nor treated with contempt nor allow His precepts to be scornfully set aside]; *for whatever a man sows, this and this only is what he will reap."* (Galatians 6:7)

In almost every instance, the sword cuts according to the seed sown. And in *every* case, *every* seed sown MUST and WILL return. According to God's Kingdom design, it is impossible for a seed not to return in manifold strength, either as a blessing or as a penalty.

The Conundrum

As Christians, we are indeed a peculiar people. We live in a fallen world but our citizenship is in Heaven. However, the moment we are born again through Jesus Christ, our eternal destiny changes. Therefore, our circumspect view of life must be according to who and what we are right now. It is this that takes us beyond the temporal age and into the eternal place with our Heavenly Father.

INTRODUCTION

"Beloved, now we are children of God, and it has not appeared as yet what we will be. We know that when He appears, we will be like Him, because we will see Him just as He is." (1 John 3:2)

Despite the promise of our great future in Jesus, we are faced with an enigma. On the one hand, we reach upward to the higher dimension of our Father's Kingdom by acknowledging His promises. But on the other hand, we are entangled with worldly attractions and distractions that offset our lives. Nonetheless, God wants you blessed beyond your imagination. For that reason, He is 100% committed in leading you to an abundant overflowing life. In order to achieve that, all things must be in divine order according to His Kingdom design.

All people are challenged, both the righteous and the unrighteous. After all, we live in a fallen world. But in every challenge, our Heavenly Father gives His children solutions.

Specific to such solutions, you are about to learn the pathway to His blessings which He established in His hidden spiritual laws. It is these very laws that govern *all* things.

The Struggles of Daily Living

In the throes of our daily struggles, Jesus gives us direct and open access to His Unshakeable Kingdom. As heirs of salvation, we have His glory. We are His, and He is ours. We are His children, not strangers. According to Jesus' Words in John 17:22, He has made us one with our Father.

> *"And the glory which You [Heavenly Father] have given Me I have given to them; that they may be one, just as We are one."* (Square brackets added by author for clarity.)

Through Jesus, we have access to our Father's unshakable promises, His immutable Word, and the splendor of His Eternal Kingdom. Since all this is true, why do some Christians live a lesser fulfilled life? Why do they struggle with limitations? Why do they *remain* sick? Why are their children plagued with strange trials? Why do entire families live in a perpetual loop of defeat along with strange unexplained occurrences in life?

INTRODUCTION

There is an answer to these mysteries. God is not deaf to the prayers of His people. After all, if we are filled with His Spirit then we are destined to be super-achievers, super-conquerors, and living fully maximized lives in power, strength, blessing, and peace. So, why the failure?

The answer is found in the hidden treasures of our Father's Word—the structure of His "Kingdom Authority". By understanding *how* His Kingdom works according to the wisdom of His spiritual laws, our limitations can be removed. None of His children must live in cycles of defeat. We are meant to soar as Eagles (Psalm 103)[1]!

To Each, a Sphere of Life

Each person occupies a unique sphere of life. Specifically speaking, each person is different. Accordingly, we have various needs, relationships, occupations, talents, skills, callings, education, intelligence, and material requirements.

What defines *your* sphere? What is *your* station and occupation—*your* calling and assignment? Whatever it is, you can have total sufficiency *and* increase in all dimensions of your life (2 Corinthians 9:8). Again, the key is understanding *how* God's Kingdom functions. Thus, by dedicating your life in pursuit of His righteousness, you can maximize your life to the full.

Do You Know the Kingdom?

Luke 16:1-13 records the parable of the cunning steward. In this story Jesus emphasized a sobering reality. Let me briefly encapsulate it for you:

A certain accountant knew he was about to lose his job. Worried about his future, he called his employer's debtors and asked how much they owed his master. One by one, the accountant adjusted the ledger to show a substantially reduced debt. Each debtor gave the steward a smile, pat on the back, and a hearty thanks.

INTRODUCTION

Exactly as he predicted, the steward lost his job. His plans, however, worked. He went back to the debtors that he helped and asked favors of them. It was dishonest in every way. But when his employer discovered the scheme, he acknowledged the steward's shrewd manipulations.

Jesus concludes this parable with an uncomfortable truth:

> *"And his master commended the unjust manager* [not for his misdeeds, but] *because he had acted shrewdly* [by preparing for his future unemployment]; *for the sons of this age* [the non-believers] *are shrewder in relation to their own kind* [that is, to the ways of the secular world] *than are the sons of light* [the Believers]." *(Luke 16:8 AMP. Square brackets added by author for clarity.)*

Even though we live in a fallen world, we who are in Jesus are *presently* citizens of our Father's unshakable Kingdom. The problem, however, is that we understand very little about our Father's immutable laws that rule over everything. We understand the "dog-eat-dog" corporate schemes of *this* world, but we are ignorant about our Father's Kingdom and how it operates. For that reason, when we encounter various besetting problems such as finances, family, health, relationships, or deliverance, we are often flummoxed as to what we should do. That is what this book is about.

Our Father's Kingdom is designed by His spiritual laws. By knowing these laws and how they operate, every sword of limitation can be removed through obedience. This, in turn, releases blessings and destroys strongholds.

What you are about to step into is something seldom taught and much less understood.

Get ready for a powerful insight that unlocks God's great and amazing blessings in your life.

Chapter One
The Spiritual Law of Creative Design

> "He is the image of the invisible God, the firstborn of all creation. 16 For by Him all things were created, both in the heavens and on earth, visible and invisible, whether thrones or dominions or rulers or authorities–all things have been created through Him and for Him. 17 He is before all things, and in Him all things hold together." (Colossians 1:15-17)

Everything in God's Kingdom functions under three specific platforms:

His laws.
His Word.
His wisdom.

According to God's purpose and plan, His *wisdom* is simply defined as the way He does whatever He does.

His *Word* is the power by which all things exist.

His *laws* are the design and operation of His Kingdom—the infrastructure by which all things function, interrelate, and harmonize according to His Word.

> "So will My Word be that goes forth out of My mouth; it will not return to Me empty without accomplishing what I desire, and without succeeding in the matter for which I sent it." (Isaiah 55:11)

The Spiritual Law of Creative Design

God's laws, Words, and wisdom never conflict one with the other. They work in a simultaneous triad of agreement to the exact intention of His will. And, they are never separated one from the other in anything that God does.

There are four operatives in everything God does. I think of them as "PPDO".

>His purpose.
>His plan.
>His design.
>His objectivity.

God doesn't experiment. He doesn't guess. He sees all things. He knows all things. He is absolute in knowledge. He knows the factor of every *cause-and-effect* that reaches in all directions throughout eternity. He is never surprised.

There is no limit to His power, nor is anything hidden from His knowledge. He does not work by mathematic probability; there is no trial and error with Him. He knows the end from the beginning. In all things, He is the final authority—not Satan. Satan has no final authority over anything throughout all of creation. This virtue belongs only to God.

STORY: My wife, Jane, is of Scottish and Lebanese descent. Her very existence is traced directly to the tragic event of the Titanic.

Celani, Jane's grandmother, was a passenger on the Titanic. She had just gotten married and was en route to America when the legendary ship struck the iceberg. Because Celani was a young female, she was permitted to have access onto one of the few lifeboats. Sadly, her husband went down with the ship.

Celani continued her journey to America. Eventually she remarried into a different Lebanese family, the "Deckers". Three generations later, Jane was born. If Celani's husband had not died, Celani would not have remarried and Jane would not exist today.

Despite the interplay of complex factors arising from that event, the truth remains that God was not surprised when Jane was born. She

The Spiritual Law of Creative Design

was not an accident. In fact, in God's omniscience, He knew her before the world was created and wrote a book about her.

✱✱✱

"My frame was not hidden from You, when I was made in secret, and skillfully wrought in the depths of the earth; 16 Your eyes have seen my unformed substance; and in Your book were all written the days that were ordained for me, when as yet there was not one of them. 17 How precious also are Your thoughts to me, O God. How vast is the sum of them! 18 If I should count them, they would outnumber the sand." (Psalm 139:15-18)

✱✱✱

Every facet of God's creation is constructed through His absolute knowledge. In His unsearchable, unfathomable, and unlimited understanding of all things, He never applies His unlimited power without first applying His unlimited wisdom.

The Laws of God

Colossians 1:16-17 describes the arrangement and design of all things created according to Jesus' wisdom.

"For by Him all things were created, both in the heavens and on earth, visible and invisible, whether thrones or dominions or rulers or authorities –all things have been created through Him and for Him. 17 <u>He is before all things, and in Him all things hold together</u>." (Underline by author for added emphasis.)

What things? "All" things in Heaven and on earth, visible and invisible, including the universe and its millions of galaxies and trillions of stars which He individually named. His creation encompasses both visible and invisible dimensions.

"He counts the number of the stars; He gives names to all of them." (Psalm 147:4)

In Jesus, *all* things are maintained and held together in their creative design. Within the tangible *natural dimension,* His immutable laws provide an orderly arrangement. Things such as gravity, aerodynamics, mathematics, and the design of the atom (to name but a few), are resolute, continuous, consistent, and unwavering.

The Spiritual Law of Creative Design

Gravity on the earth does not vary. The flittering sparrows and the elite fighter jets fly by the same aerodynamic laws.

Laws of the spiritual realm are just as real and unwavering: laws of sowing and reaping; continuity; harmony; pairing; confession; alignment; separation; agreement; faith; redemption; forgiveness; and so forth.

> **A person living under the curse of unforgiven sins will struggle with diminished levels of success, minimized blessing, and unattainable lasting peace.**

All things are designed in an orderly, harmonious, interrelated network of *cause-and-effect*. They are governed by "authorities" or "rulers" which the Bible calls "spiritual and natural laws"—the invisible ordinances that Jesus spoke into existence when He created all things (Romans 13:1-4).

You can't see the wind, but you can see its effect. In the same way, you can't see God's spiritual laws, but you can see their effect. They are an ever present force. They are untiring, consistent, immutable, without variance, unbiased, and they superintend all things.

The *spiritual* realm governs the *natural* realm. If anyone violates God's spiritual laws (referred to as "rulers, authorities, and ordinances"), it produces a sword—an unavoidable consequence.

Forgiveness is a spiritual law. In Mark 11: 26, it says:

> *"But if you do not forgive, neither will your Father who is in Heaven forgive your transgressions."*

An unforgiving person brings a sword against their own life. They have diminished levels of success and vacillating peace. Until he or she obeys **The Spiritual Laws of Forgiveness**, a sword is set against them. Consequently, their ongoing failures remain mysteriously

The Spiritual Law of Creative Design

weaved into various sectors of their life.[2] The sin of refusing to forgive others is this: holding unforgiveness imprisons the "unforgiver" to *all* their sins.

In *almost* every case, generational curses have limited power. Simply stated, a curse is the sword's action based on violations of God's spiritual laws. Generally, God limits the sword to no more than the 3rd and 4th generation. Therefore, Christians seldom need to consider generational curses beyond the 4th generation.

When God revealed His character to Moses, He declared the statute of limitation:

> *"Then the Lord passed by in front of him [Moses] and proclaimed, 'The Lord, the Lord God, compassionate and gracious, slow to anger, and abounding in lovingkindness and truth; 7 yet He will by no means leave the guilty unpunished, visiting the iniquity of the father on the children and on the grandchildren to the third and fourth generation." (Exodus 34:6-7. Square brackets added by author for clarity.)*

There are, however, a few exceptions to this law. Depending on the offense, some swords perpetually link from one generation to the next. For example, Eli was a priest in Israel. However, His sons acted without holy regard for the Lord's honor while they performed their priestly duties. Even worse, Eli did not respect God by correcting his wayward sons. As a result, in 1 Samuel 2:29-30, God said of Eli's house:

> *"Why do you kick at My sacrifice and at My offering which I have commanded in My dwelling, and honor your sons above Me, by making yourselves fat with the choicest of every offering of My people Israel?' 30 Therefore the LORD God of Israel declares, 'I did indeed say that your house and the house of your father should walk before Me forever'; but now the LORD declares, 'Far be it from Me--for those who honor Me I will honor, and those who*

---

[2] A curse employs a supernatural power that inflicts harm or punishment on someone or something.

The Spiritual Law of Creative Design

despise Me will be lightly esteemed. Therefore I have sworn to the house of Eli that the iniquity of Eli's house shall not be atoned for by sacrifice or offering forever." (1 Samuel 3:14)

Samuel was raised by Eli who was not his biological father. However, Eli's model as a father influenced Samuel's practice of fatherhood. But unlike Eli, Samuel was not derelict in addressing his (Samuel's) sons. However, Samuel's sons chose not to walk in their father's ways. For this reason, when Samuel was old and his governance over Israel was ending, the Israelites asked for a king. Instead of being ruled by God's appointed judges and prophets, they wanted a leader like the surrounding nations. Their request was directly influenced by Samuel's failure within his own house. To that effect, they said to him:

> *"Behold, you have grown old and your sons do not walk in your ways. Now appoint a king for us to judge us like all the nations."*
> (1 Samuel 8:5)

What happened between Samuel and his sons? Spiritual laws came into play. There is no mention of them acting like the sons of Eli, but for whatever reason, they did not identify with their father's calling. Consequently, because they were not **spiritually aligned** with him, they failed to receive Samuel's spiritual inheritance.

Spoken Curses

Curses are sometimes decreed through dark personalities such as tribal witchdoctors, fetish priests, shamans, or those standing in spiritual authority that invoke demonic interplay.

STORY: In one particular African village, the region saw no rain for four years. The land was desolate and dry and the people suffered greatly. A young girl on her first missionary trip came to the village and learned of the witchdoctor's curse. Even though he died several years earlier, the power of his curse remained. As the missionary stood looking at the parched land, the Lord told her to take a carafe of water, and while calling on the name of the Lord, pour it upon the ground and rebuke the curse spoken by the witchdoctor. That same day the rains began.

The Spiritual Law of Creative Design

STORY: Kenneth Hagin, a prophet and teacher, was asked by a father and mother to come to the hospital and pray for their son who was thirty-nine years old and lay in a deep coma.

On the way there, the Lord spoke to Kenneth and said, "There is nothing you can do for him. Spiritual laws are in motion that cannot be reversed." Kenneth did not know exactly which laws, but he went to the hospital to comfort the family.

While talking to the mother, she said, "You know, from the time he was a young boy, he always said he would never live to the age of forty."

There it was: By reckless repetitive confessions, the man assigned a destiny to himself. Because he lay in a coma, he could not repent for such confessions and cancel the curse through repentance.

★★★

The Spiritual Law of Confession is an invisible spiritual law. In the above case, the young man ignorantly set laws into motion. He was the only one that could remove the sword by repentance and forgiveness.

> "Death and life are in the **power of the tongue**, and those who love it will eat its fruit." (Proverbs 18:21)

> "For by your **words** you will be acquitted, and by your words you will be condemned." (Matthew 12:37)

> "An evil man is trapped by his **rebellious speech**, but a righteous man escapes from trouble." (Proverbs 12:13)

> "He who **guards his mouth** protects his life, but the one who opens his lips invites his own ruin." (Proverbs 13:3)

> "He who **guards his mouth** and tongue, keeps his soul from distress." (Proverbs 21:23)

As a former career police officer, I frequently saw the sword's penalty in people's lives. It showed by how they think; their repeated patterns of behavior; their words; their actions; wrong decisions linked in

The Spiritual Law of Creative Design

continual patterns of thought—all contrary to the truth. Consequently, the parent's swords passed to the children who practiced the same values. It is a generational curse that produces the same outcomes: the grandfather was a criminal who raised a criminal son that went to prison, who also raised sons that went to prison.

Sadly, those caught in the dismal cycles of destruction believe that their parent's failure is the same destiny they have as well—it is their *normal*. It is what they expect.

When negative ongoing factors continually occur, somewhere there is a sword. Until one recognizes the sword, confesses their sins, repents, and aligns with God's righteousness, the sword remains active. But how can they repent if they don't understand the spiritual laws of God's Kingdom? The only answer is Jesus. If they turn to Him, the sword can be identified and removed.

Because of ignorance, many Christians never achieve higher dimensions in their spiritual walk. To them, living a defeated life is normal.

Such Christians are easily recognized. They are spiritually fatigued. Their souls are wounded and broken. They fight the same battles over, and over, and over. They are grooved in the same mindsets, values, words, and expectations that move in cycles. They laterally shift, but never advance forward. They stay busy, but never increase. Their forward progress is stopped. True are the words of Hosea who said God's people are destroyed through lack of knowledge.

> *"My people are destroyed for lack of knowledge."* (Hosea 4:6a)

A person might have success in one area of life, but live defeated in other areas that suppresses their advancement. Until they find the root-problem and understand God's spiritual laws, there will always be a failure to launch because of the *limiter*—the sword. Consequently, they learn to accept defeat and adjust their lives to the levels of its limit.

> *"Like a sparrow in its flitting, like a swallow in its flying, so a curse without a cause does not alight."* (Proverbs 26:2)

The Spiritual Law of Creative Design

An Unchangeable Kingdom

According to John 1:3, Jesus created all things. All things came into existence through Him, and apart from Him, nothing exists.

> *"Through Him all things were made; without Him nothing was made that has been made."*

By Jesus' power, all things are held together in a stable unalterable state of existence exactly as He designed them. God's Kingdom is therefore unchangeable, unshakable, consistent, and subject only to Him.

When behavior remains unchanged, people are destined to the same repetitive outcomes which links from generation to generation.

A miracle is when God sets aside His natural laws and by His spiritual laws performs the impossible. The Bible records such miracles such as when Jesus walked on water; or when He fed 5,000 people by re-generating a few fish and loaves of bread; or when He turned water into wine; or when He sent manna from Heaven; or when He instantly translated His disciples in the middle of the Sea of Galilee to the shore—to name just a few.

Aren't We Redeemed From the Curse of the Law?

Paul, who wrote the book of Romans, clearly understood God's spiritual laws. In Romans 8:2, he explains two of them:

> *"For the law of the Spirit of life in Christ Jesus has set you free from the law of sin and of death."*

Those in Jesus Christ live under **The Law of the Spirit of Life**; and those who are unsaved, live under **The Law of Sin and Death**.

Two spiritual laws. Two classifications of people.

Those living under **The Law of Sin and Death** are condemned until they receive Jesus Christ as their Lord and Savior.

The Spiritual Law of Creative Design

And those living under **The Law of the Spirit of Life** have eternal life with full access to our Father's Kingdom.

The privilege and power of "sonship" comes through **The Law of the Spirit of Life** in Jesus Christ. Hence, we are sons, not slaves. As sons, our Father entitles us to His Kingdom resources! We have His Word, His blessings, and His supernatural intervention in our lives.

Because we are God's children, our Father is 100% committed to removing every sword from our history. His loving intention is to give us a life free of swords—abundantly and overflowing. To achieve this, We must recognize and obey His spiritual laws.

Jesus Redeemed Us

Even though Jesus redeemed us from the *curse* of the law, the spiritual laws that govern His Kingdom remain in full force. Without them, God's Kingdom has no structure or consistency. Therefore, understanding their function is vital.

God's spiritual laws regulate the infrastructure of His Kingdom. Because all things are subject to them, they never change. All of our blessings and advancements come through these laws. For instance, in our Father's Kingdom, **The Law of Sin and Death** and **The Law of the Spirit of Life** are two primary laws. These laws define two domains under which all people are classified. Each person exists in one or the other.

People that are classified under **The Law of Sin and Death** are eternally condemned unless they receive Jesus Christ as their Lord and Savior. In contrast, people that are classified under **The Law of the Spirit of Life** have been granted eternal life in Jesus Christ and are made children of our Heavenly Father.

> "But Christ has rescued us from the curse pronounced by the law. When he was hung on the cross, he took upon himself the curse for our wrongdoing. For it is written in the Scriptures, "Cursed is everyone who is hung on a tree." *(Galatian 3:13, New Living Translation)*

Before Jesus saved us, we were under **The Law of Sin and Death** and our spirits were dead. By receiving Jesus, we are born again and made

The Spiritual Law of Creative Design

alive according to **The Law of the Spirit of Life**. He translated us from death into life by a spiritual law. Then He delivered us from a *sin nature* by making us alive in Him through another spiritual law.

To emphasize the point, before and after salvation, we are subject to God's spiritual laws of creation. They remain perpetually in force to ensure an immutable, unshakable, and unchangeable Kingdom through our Savior.

Satan is powerless to change God's spiritual laws. Therefore, he can only exploit them. For instance, **The Spiritual Law of Sowing and Reaping** says that whatever a person sows, they will reap. Satan knows that every seed brings a harvest. And, he knows God cannot bless unrighteousness. Therefore he tempts people into sowing unrighteousness in order to produce the sword of penalty.

To "Know" God

By God's Spirit, we are taught His immutable Word. Therefore, in order to correctly apply His laws, we must apply them by our Father's wisdom. By understanding His wisdom, we can move from blessing to blessing by obedience.

> **Jesus redeemed us from the "curse" of law that ends in spiritual death, that is, the moral and ethical laws. But He did not deliver anyone or anything from His spiritual laws.**

> *"To know wisdom and instruction, to discern the sayings of understanding. 3 To receive instructions in wise behavior, righteousness, justice, and equity; 4 to give prudence to the naïve, to the youth knowledge and discretion. 5 A wise man will hear and increase in learning, and a man of understanding will acquire wise counsel."* (Proverbs 1:1-5)

Now, with all certainty, no one has fully comprehended the infinite depths of God's wisdom and ways. The Apostle Paul made this point quite clear:

The Spiritual Law of Creative Design

"Oh, the depth and the riches both of wisdom and knowledge of God! How unsearchable [unlimited] *are His judgments and unfathomable His ways."* (Romans 11:33. *Square brackets added by author for clarity.)*

While God's wisdom is infinite and unfathomable, the Spirit of Truth and Revelation—the Holy Spirit—reveals our Heavenly Father's wisdom for every need in our lives. He leads us into abundant living with overflowing success through His immutable Word.

In the next chapter, we'll look at our Father's Kingdom Authority through the lens of Romans 13:1-4, one of the most misapplied and misunderstood area of Scripture.

Chapter Two
The Spiritual Law of Governing Authorities

"**Every person is to be in subjection to the governing authorities. For there is no authority except from God. And those which exist are established by God. 2 Therefore whoever resists authority has opposed the ordinance of God, and they who have opposed will receive condemnation upon themselves. 3 For rulers are not a cause of fear for good behavior, but for evil. Do you want to have no fear of authority? Do what is good and you will have praise from the same, 4 for _it_ is a minister of God to you for good. But if you do what is evil, be afraid; for _it_ does not bear the sword for nothing; for _it_ is a minister of God, an avenger who brings wrath on the one who practices evil.**" (Romans 13:1-4 Underlie by author for emphasis.)

Depending upon which Bible translation you use, the above verse can be very conflicting. For example, the New International Version, New King James Version, and the King James version, designates the words, *governing authorities,* as being "people in authority" by using the pronoun "he" in verse four. This would mean that certain people are empowered by government such as soldiers and police officers, including officials that make and enforce laws, which in that sense, is true.

However, the New American Standard version (predominately used throughout this book), renders a more accurate translation. It defines

The Spiritual Law of Governing Authorities

governing authority as an *immutable unchanging force* rather than a person delegated with authority. Thus, in verse four, The New American Standard uses the word "it", not the word "he", when referring to authority. By the correct use of this simple pronoun, everything in the passage changes meaning.

God's Word is a *force of power,* an imputable ever-present sentinel throughout His Kingdom that rules over all things. The root of His creation is His Word. All things are subject to *the power of His Word.* Those who obey His laws *benefit* from the power in His Word which produces life-giving positive change.

> *"So shall My word be that goes forth from My mouth; it shall not return to Me void, but it shall accomplish what I please, and it shall prosper in the thing for which I sent it."* (Isaiah 55:11)

Obedience releases blessing. Conversely, those who violate God's laws suffer by *penalty rather than advance by blessing.* According to verse four, authority comes as a sword of vengeance. This is immutable. There is no flex, variance, or vacillation. It is either blessing for obedience, or a sword for disobedience.

Civil or Spiritual; Absolute or Provisional

Romans 13:1-4 either requires absolute obedience to *authority* or it does not. Therefore, the subject of "authority" in Romans 13:1-4 must be defined. Is it *God's authority* by His laws, or does Romans mean *man's authority* by man's laws?

The truth is, nothing in the wording of Romans 13:1-4 allows us to disobey God's governing authorities. There is nothing in the wording that give anyone this privilege. If, however, people interpret *governing authority* as people presiding over government positions, then conflicts immediately arise. Some feel Romans 13:1-4 means conditional compliance. And if it does, then we no longer have universal agreement. Each person has their own interpretation.

Let me further explain how this works: God's Word is an absolute moral truth. This means there is no variation; no off-angle application; and no gray areas. Obedience is required at all times, not most

The Spiritual Law of Governing Authorities

of the time, and not by situational application. It is not up for self-interpretation or applied according to custom, culture, or tradition. His Word cannot be modified by personal choice, or set aside by changing political and cultural values.

However, if Romans 13:1-4 requires submission to people in governing positions, then America is cursed because it was founded upon sin. The pioneers of America rebelled against the king of England—a government in authority. America fought a bloody resistance called "The Revolutionary War"—a revolt against established authority!

Further:

- The Apostles rebelled against the authority of the temple leaders who ordered them not to preach the name of Jesus.

- 800,000 Christians rebelled against the pope by refusing to give allegiance to him and his Church that had both spiritual *and* governmental authority over them.

- Christians and Jews rebelled against Hitler's governmental authority which resulted in mass murder and persecution.

- The coming Antichrist is a global authority where over one-fourth of mankind stands against him and are subsequently killed.

"If" the intended meaning of Romans 13:1-4 requires Christians to obey people in government positions of authority, then we are frequently conflicted between God's absolute truth and man's sinful laws such as the LGBTQ+ agenda. One person has this opinion and another person has that opinion. One culture licenses prostitution while another culture executes prostitutes. Obviously, Romans 13:1-4 can't be interpreted according to every whim of man's laws.

Therefore, Christians that believe Romans 13:1-4 means obedience to people in government positions of authority, must modify God's Word with personalized clauses of exceptions. But, according to the accurate interpretation of these verses, it is not permitted. Thus, when the privilege to obey laws and ordinances are based on each person's opinion, then Romans 13:1-4 cannot be a moral absolute truth. In such cases, every person assumes the privilege to obey or

The Spiritual Law of Governing Authorities

disobey according to their own conscience, political view, and personal tenets of religion.

David Barton, founder of Wallbuilders, a national organization that preserves America's forgotten history and heroes with an emphasis on moral, religious, and constitutional heritage says this:

> "Current polling shows that two out of three Americans believe there is no absolute moral truth; four out of five millennials believe there is no moral absolute truth, and even one out of two Christians believe there is no moral absolute truth. So truth is now determined individually; it's determined by "my" agenda; it's determined by what "I" want to get done. That leads exactly to what we're starting to see now. Three times in the Bible; twice in the book of Judges it says: 'Every man did that which was right in his own eyes.' So we are now Machiavellian, and the end justifies the means. This is a real problem when you no longer have morals that are right and wrong. We've seen this coming. We've called it situational ethics back thirty years ago, and then we got into what is moral liberaltarianism where you can't tell me what is right and wrong; I'll decide for myself."[3]

All of God's Word is founded upon absolute truth. It is without ambiguity. Thus, when Romans 13:1-4 is based on God's spiritual laws, the subject of "authority" is accurately interpreted as a "divine power of God" instead of "people in governing positions of authority". In the proper interpretation, all vacillations, inconsistencies, and subjective choices are eliminated.

Being in "subjection" to authority means to yield to, obey, or voluntarily put one's self in willful compliance. If we view God's Word as THE ultimate ruling authority, then obedience is without conflict because His Word fits all generations for all time in every culture of all nations. Consequently, the personal prerogative to obey or disobey leaders and their laws is completely eliminated.

---

[3] (David Barton, Founder:Wallbuilders.com)

The Spiritual Law of Governing Authorities

The Sword

"But if you do what is evil, be afraid; for it does not bear the sword for nothing; for it is a minister of God, an avenger who brings wrath on the one who practices evil." (Romans 13:4a)
"Therefore, repent; or else I am coming to you quickly, and I will make war against them with the sword of My mouth."
(Revelation 2:16)

Referring again to Colossians and the Gospel of John, everything that exists came into being when Jesus "spoke" His Word. Peter affirms this truth where he says:

"By the Word of God, the heavens existed long ago, and the earth was formed out of water and by water." (2 Peter 3:5b)

When Jesus spoke His Word, everything was made in the precise order and design according to the exact intention of His will. Only His Word was required—nothing else. Therefore, when He spoke His Word, blessings and penalties; promotions and boundaries; checks and balances; and domains and governances were weaved into His Kingdom which includes His spiritual laws. We are blessed if we obey His Word, and if we disobey, we incur the penalty of a sword.

In the design of God's Kingdom, the sword's penalty comes on the cause of disobedience. Equally as true are the blessings which come by obedience. If there were no penalty connected with disobedience, God's Kingdom would collapse to the works of darkness. The sword, in this regard, is an avenger against all who practice evil. It sets boundaries and checks the progress of evil.

Understanding Romans 13:1-4

"Every person is to be in subjection to the governing authorities (vs1).*"* The governing authorities in this passage are God's spiritual and natural "laws" which Jesus integrated throughout His creation. It is these very laws which superintend all things as rulers acting as an unbiased governing immutable force. They consistently operate in righteousness to guarantee blessings *and* arrest evil. Therefore, if anyone violates His laws, the sword's penalty automatically comes as a regulating judgment.

The Spiritual Law of Governing Authorities

The effects of sowing and reaping is a spiritual law. One who sows to the flesh, reaps from that domain. And one who sows to the spirit, reaps from that domain. It never varies. Every seed produces according to its kind—it is an immutable spiritual law.

If one routinely exercises, he or she will reap the benefits of great health. If one spends time in reckless eating, he or she will reap the detriments of poor health. Every action is a seed that produces a harvest. This is a spiritual law.

When we sow what is right, good, and wholesome, God's spiritual laws ensure blessings. Simply stated: life flourishes in accordance with His Word and His Word never varies in truth.

The Spiritual Law of Implied Reverse

Based on **The Spiritual Law of the Implied Reverse**, the opposite of righteousness is sin. Sin produces penalties—every time, no exception. For example, if anyone refuses to forgive others, the same person is not forgiven. *All* of their sins are a sword set against their life. In the absence of God's grace and mercy, the sword devours. Moreover, recognizing the sword's effect in correlation to a particular violation of God's spiritual laws is sometimes difficult. This is because God's spiritual laws are an a unyielding, immutable, and unbiased force.

> "See to it that <u>no one comes short of the grace of God</u>; that no root of bitterness springing up causes trouble, and by it many be defiled." *(Hebrews 12:15. Underline by author for added emphasis.)*

Satan takes no prisoners. He has no conscience. He does not care how a person slips into disobedience, whether by deliberate action, ignorance, or confusion. He knows that God's spiritual laws work without variance for any cause or reason. They are consistent and unstoppable.

Satan takes no prisoners. He has no conscience. Whether a person violates God's laws by ignorance or rebellion, Satan does not care how or why it happens.

The Spiritual Law of Governing Authorities

"For there is no authority except from God. And those which exist are established by God (vs1b)*."* The Word is quite plain: God's creation perfectly reflects His righteousness in all things of truth without conflict. This is based on **The Spiritual Law of Continuity**. Accordingly, God does nothing that will ever violate or contradict His own character.

After He created the Heavens and the earth, five times He said it was "good" (Genesis 1: 10, 12, 18, 21, 25). This assessment included the hidden spiritual laws that rule, govern, and regulate His creation pertaining to both blessings and penalties.

"Therefore, whoever resists authority has opposed the ordinance of God, and they who have opposed will receive condemnation upon themselves (vs2)*."* God's Word produces life. Sin produces death. These are unchanging absolutes. They are inalterable absolutes according to God's spiritual laws. Death is a spiritual law to all who deny Jesus. In the same way, life is a spiritual law to all who accept Jesus. Sin cannot promote life, and obedience cannot produce death.

EXAMPLE: The Chinese Bamboo is utterly remarkable. After it is planted, nothing happens for four to five years. Even if it is watered and fertilized, there is no evidence of growth. Its life remains hidden, still, and soon forgotten.

On or around the fifth year, something occurs. It breaks dormancy and in six weeks grows to a height of ninety feet! This species of bamboo has been known to grow as much as forty-eight inches in a 24-hour period, and sometimes up to thirty-nine inches in a single hour for short periods of time!

The effect of righteousness or sin is very similar. The seeds may seem dormant. Nonetheless, they are very much alive and are time-dated for harvest.

✸✸✸

"Let us not lose heart in doing good, for in due time we will reap if we do not grow weary." (Galatians 6:9)

The Spiritual Law of Governing Authorities

In like manner, the sword always manifests in the exact context of its due time. It is **The Spiritual Law of the Seed**. Even though it lies dormant, like the Chinese Bamboo, it suddenly comes into action.

STORY: A particular ranking officer that I worked with was known for his criminal behavior. Because he was the assistant chief, no one wanted to take action against him. Aside from that, he was well liked throughout the community by those who considered the claims as nothing more than rumor. However, several officers took him to task and investigated his nefarious activities which include thefts from the department, illegal gun running, and his plethora of opportunistic thefts from various businesses when an unguarded open door was discovered after operational hours. In one investigation, he was caught embezzling department funds and was required to pay back the missing money. This, however, merely resulted in a few days of suspension. Over time, he amassed a significant amount of personal property, houses, a mountain cabin, in addition to a collection of stolen guns.

He was a mean vicious person that used the advantage of his rank to oppress officers who refused to be intimidated by him. Reports soon filtered up to the courts and his credibility as an officer was completely debunked. Ultimately, the man retired. His plans were set to enjoy his life which he fashioned and constructed from his crimes.

I asked the Lord one day how a man who displaced the lives of so many career officers and who built his wealth from stolen items could remain unscathed. In prayer, the Lord told me these specific words: "I gave him time to repent and to make restitution but he would not. He is now judged."

Within three days, the man was working on the roof of his mountain cabin when he was suddenly struck dead by a massive heart attack. He fell three stories from his roof onto the slope below. Based on the posture of his body lying on the ground, investigators determined that he was dead before he hit the ground.

His life was over in an instant. In all that he had amassed for his retirement, he never had a chance to enjoy it. His sin was hidden in the ground while God waited for him to repent. Because he had grown

The Spiritual Law of Governing Authorities

callous and indifferent, he made no such effort. In the due season, like the Chinese bamboo, suddenly the sword came due.

The only thing that STOPS the sword is: (1) confessing the sin to both God and man; (2) repentance by aligning with God's Word; and (3) restitution where required. From that point forward, the penalty stops and blessings begin. Nonetheless, even with the sword removed, the government action of sin still continues. (This is explained in Chapter 4.)

> *"For rulers are not a cause of fear for good behavior, but for evil. Do you want to have no fear of authority? Do what is good and you will have praise from the same, 4 for it is a minister of God to you for good." (Romans 13:3. Underline by author for added emphasis.)*

The design of God's spiritual laws ensure our blessings by obedience—blessings that are equally as absolute and certain as the penalties for disobedience. The *rulers* (His spiritual laws), cannot be annulled by Satan or put away. However, Satan can prevent blessings by coercing one into disobedience through the lust of the eyes; the lust of the flesh, and the pride of life.

Rulers

What are these "rulers" that are mentioned in Romans 13:3? Are they people or personalities?

They are not people. Rather, they are God's hidden spiritual laws that rule and govern all things. His laws are infused with power and authority. They regulate according to the seed sown, either by righteousness or by disobedience. They work by a *cause-and-effect* outcome.

The word, "RULER" is a Greek word, "archon" and means first in rank or power. It can sometimes refer to people in governing authority, such as a king. But the context used in Romans 13 pertains to God's laws and ordinances—the visible and invisible laws that "rule" and govern over ALL things. (See 1 Peter 2:12-16.)

Again, if Romans 13:1-4 is interpreted as *people of governing authority*, then it cannot be an absolute moral truth. For example, if

The Spiritual Law of Governing Authorities

Christians submit to "rulers" as being people who make evil laws, then God's people would be required to align with things God hates. Again, this violates **The Spiritual Law of Continuity** where God does nothing that conflicts with His own character.

Thus, if Romans 13:1-4 requires that we obey *all* people in governing positions, then it cannot be a moral absolute. As a result, each person's interpretation is according to their culture, conscience, and opinion. Based on such variables, there is no universal agreement on the standard of truth when it comes to applying Romans 13:1-4.

No person in any position of governing authority has preeminence over God's laws and ordinances. Rather, every person and personality, both in the heavens and on earth, are subject to God's "rulers"—His laws and ordinances.

Of course, in order to obey God's laws, we must first know and understand them. And in order to properly apply them, we must have His wisdom.

Apart from God's Word, conscience is shaped largely by environmental and cultural values. For this reason, the Woke Generation is universally bankrupt. "Wokers" are immersed in a dark satanic philosophy. Lacking God's wisdom and righteousness, they do not know how to apply equality according to truth. For that reason, they cast truth aside and each person has their own philosophy of right and wrong.

God's Kingdom is not subject to cultural values. His righteousness never changes; His truths never vary. His Word is absolute for all generations at all times.

> *"But if you do what is evil* [as defined by God], *be afraid; for it* [God's power of authority] *does not bear the sword for nothing; for **it** is a minister of God, an avenger who brings wrath on the one who practices evil."* (Romans 13:4 . Square brackets added by author for clarity.

The standard of truth is this: anything contrary to God's righteousness is evil. He is the fountainhead, the originator of all truth and righteousness—the standard by which all things are gauged.

The Spiritual Law of Governing Authorities

According to **The Spiritual Law of Continuity**, God's love, Word, truth, righteousness, and character never conflict one with the other.

He established His laws and set boundaries for all things. His laws (rulers) act as a vigilant fast-moving force within the tenets and design of His creation. For this reason, His sword cuts with absolute certainty and exact precision every single time. No exceptions.

What Do We Do With Civil Obedience?

This subject is addressed in 1 Peter 2:12-16 and specifically deals with our public Christian testimony. Based on the context of words used in this Scripture, God grants discretion:

> *"Keep your behavior excellent among the Gentiles, so that in the thing in which they slander you as evildoers, they may because of your good deeds, as they observe them, glorify God on the day of visitation. 13 Submit yourselves for the Lord's sake to every human institution, whether to a king as the one in authority 14 or to governors as sent by him for the punishment of evildoers and the praise of those who do right. 15 For such is the will of God, that by doing right you silence the ignorance of foolish people. 16 Act as free people, and do not use your freedom as a covering for evil, but use it as bond-servants of God."*

The application of 1 Peter 2:12-16 is different from Romans 13:1-4. Peter addresses *conditional limited compliance* to civil authorities with clear admonitions.

"Evildoers" are defined according to God's righteousness, not man's values. The implied sense of any government punishing "evildoers" first assumes that the government's position is morally consistent with God's Kingdom values.

STORY: When Covid-19 débuted in 2020, the world reeled in panic. People died at an alarming rate and no one knew what to do. Fear saturated societies all over the world. Governments were terrified. People acted irrationally. I had just returned from Africa and learned there was a rush on toilet paper in the United States. How abstract.

The Spiritual Law of Governing Authorities

Greed, money, and power always exploit people's fear. Governments rushed to find a vaccine and implemented unreasonable and ridiculous mandates such as six-foot spacing and non-medical grade face masks that did nothing at all to prevent the spread of disease. After walking into a restaurant and sitting down, face masks could be removed. Adding to the hysteria, there were prohibitions against public gatherings. Churches shut down and went to live streaming.

I came before the Lord and asked what we should do. His Word was clear: "Carry on. Change nothing. Set a spiritual canopy in place."

On Sunday, I told the church we were not shutting down; we would not require masks; and there would be no six-foot spacing. We would carry on as usual—laying hands on sick people, anointing them with oil, praying in their homes, having fellowship dinners, etcetera.

It was an interesting outcome. **The Spiritual Law of the Canopy** proved itself again (see Chapter Nine). There were no casualties, and no one went to the hospital. However, three people that *formerly* had attended the church became sick with Covid-19. Each was fear-based—the very ones that were vaccinated and stayed away from church for nearly three months.

I found no violation of conscience when ignoring the government mandates. Should I be a hypocrite and ignore God's promises found in Psalm 91? Did not the Lord address these issues in His Word? Was I to be a preacher of His Word, but run like a coward when it came to standing in faith? For me, NOT trusting God's Word and complying with fear was a moral violation:

> *"You will not be afraid of the terror by night, or of the arrow that flies by day; 6 of the pestilence that stalks in darkness, or of the destruction that lays waste at noon. 7 A thousand may fall at your side and ten thousand at your right hand, but it shall not approach you." (Psalm 91:5-7)*

Covid-19 was a dress rehearsal for the Body of Christ. It revealed each person's faith-walk. Sadly, an overwhelming percentage of Christians were moved more by fear than by faith. They discovered that their trust in God's Word was nothing more than a philosophical mental concession. To them, Psalms 91 was just another religious ideology.

The Spiritual Law of Governing Authorities

Fear-filled Christians found no value in church fellowship. Yet, they went to work; they went shopping; they continued their daily routines, but they were fearful to come to church and sit shoulder to shoulder.

If we *believe* God's Word and promises, why was there fear? Why did so many Christians line up for the vaccine—a failed untested serum which is now responsible for untold numbers of medical complications and sudden deaths?

Why did Christians put their hope in man rather than the Lord? Why did they rush into the unknown of man's methods, but avoid absolute trust upon God's unchanging promises?

Did man's laws work? No. Did masses of people submit to them? Yes. Were the Covid-19 mandates Constitutional? No. Repetitive court cases have upheld the defendants, not the government.

> "The country [Israel] has one of the world's highest covid-19 vaccination levels, with about 78 percent of those ages 12 and older fully vaccinated, mostly with the Pfizer vaccine. At the same time, Israel now has the highest infection rate in the world, potentially a sign of waning vaccine immunity as the highly contagious delta variant spreads. *Science* Reports."[4]

Many people who received the covid-19 vaccination have since suffered strange sicknesses and even death from it. Further, even though many were triple vaccinated, it proved to be of no effect against covid-19. In fact, the covid-19 vaccination has caused vast numbers of debilitating physical issues ranging from miscarriages, severe and massive blood clotting, and surges of adult deaths.

***

Without objection, Christians *should* obey civil laws and government authorities by showing "good behavior". Good behavior means righteous acts as first defined by *God's righteousness*. The civil laws implied in 1 Peter 2:12-16 suggest they are not in conflict with the Lord's

---

[4] Israel is one of the most fully covid 19 vaccinated nations in the world at nearly 100% of its population. https://www.beckershospitalreview.com/public-health/nearly-60-of-hospitalized-covid-19-patients-in-israel-fully-vaccinated-study-finds.html

The Spiritual Law of Governing Authorities

righteousness because those in authority are punishing "evildoers". Evildoers are those opposed to God's righteousness. Therefore, compliance with any law first implies that the law is righteous.

1 Peter 2:12-16 cannot apply to every human institution or it would also apply to the rule and reign of Antichrist when he commands everyone to receive his mark, make an image of him, and worship it. This is an unforgiveable sin resulting in eternal damnation. Therefore, rightly dividing the word of truth is required when applying 1 Peter 2:12-16 as compared to Romans 13:1-4.

> *"Be diligent to present yourself approved as a workman who does not need to be ashamed, accurately handling the Word of Truth."*
> *(2 Timothy 2:15)*

Again, the difference between Romans 13:1-4 and 1 Peter 2:12-16 is context. Romans addresses spiritual laws; Peter addresses civil laws.

Chapter Three
The Spiritual Law of Sowing and Reaping

"Do not be deceived. God is not mocked; for whatever a man sows, this he will also reap. 8 For the one who sows to his own flesh from the flesh will reap corruption, but the one who sows to the Spirit will from the Spirit reap eternal life." (Galatians 6:7-8)

The Apostle Peter set forth a clear explanation of God's intentions for all who are in Christ:

> "Grace and peace be multiplied to you in the knowledge of God and of Jesus our Lord; seeing that His divine power has granted to us everything pertaining to life and godliness through the true knowledge of Him who called us by His own glory and excellence. For by these, He has granted to us His precious and magnificent promises, so that by them you may become partakers of the divine nature, having escaped the corruption that is in the world through lust." (2 Peter 1:2-4)

Grace and peace comes *through the revelation-knowledge* of God our Father and of Jesus our Lord. It implies that everything is granted to us through "obedience" by first understanding the intimate workings of His ways, laws, and ordinances.

The Spiritual Law of Sowing and Reaping

According to the sphere of life we occupy, the design of God's Kingdom contains everything we need. But it is our obedience that unlocks the treasures of His spiritual laws.

His spiritual laws run parallel with His moral and ethical laws. Keep in mind, however, God's spiritual laws are the infrastructure of His creation. They apply to everyone and everything, in all places, at all times, without exceptions.

> **If God's spiritual laws are annulled by the sacrifice of Jesus' death, then the spiritual laws designed to bless us are cancelled as well.**

As previously mentioned, Jesus never suspends or sets aside His governing spiritual laws. If being saved exempts us from such laws, then the spiritual laws that ensure our blessings are cancelled as well. Moreover, there would be no Kingdom structure, nothing absolute, nothing consistent, and nothing to act on in faith.

In contrast, Satan prefers a kingdom without laws, structures, or design—a kingdom where everyone does what is right in their own eyes; a Kingdom without moral absolutes. Therefore, it is not surprising that Satan's woke philosophy seeks to eliminate gender distinctiveness where each person identifies according to what they want to be and not what they actually are.

To be perfectly clear, Jesus delivered His people from the eternal penalty of death. But before and after any person's salvation, His spiritual laws always remain.

Based on our Father's Kingdom laws, how shall we access His blessings? The answer is simple, but it requires tenacious effort. We must study God's Word and subject ourselves to the Holy Spirit as He imparts revelation, understanding, and insight. Only He can do this for us. Only He knows the mind and wisdom of our Father's Kingdom. In this regard, we are told:

> *"Wisdom is the principle thing. Therefore, get wisdom and all your getting, get understanding."* (Proverbs 4:7)

The Spiritual Law of Sowing and Reaping

By God's Word, He integrated the network of His spiritual laws and ordinances into His creation. If His laws could be annulled, everything in creation would cease to function because there would be nothing according to **The Spiritual Law of Continuity**.

Knowing His spiritual laws is the first step. The second step is understanding them. The third step is acquiring God's wisdom in order to properly apply them.

Fused Operations

As represented in the metaphor of the seed, there are three primary spiritual laws which govern all things that are detailed in Chapter Six of Part II in this book:

>The law of the seed-type.
>The law of sowing and reaping.
>The law of manifold return.

God binds Himself to His unchangeable Word. He is His Word, and His Word is Him. Because He never changes, we have assurance in everything He says. The power of our faith joins in agreement with the power of His immutable Word. Through obedience, we receive His blessings. It is that simple.

>**To be perfectly clear, Jesus delivered His people from the eternal penalty of sin. But before and after we are saved, His spiritual laws remain in full force.**

Prosperous people live according to God's spiritual laws. It is not a mystery. His laws produce success and abundance to both Believers and Unbelievers. God's spiritual laws, therefore, act without bias.

Even blessed people have problems. After all, we live in a fallen world. But, because of God's spiritual laws, we have workable solutions in every circumstance.

The Spiritual Law of Sowing and Reaping

Equally so, people who rebel against God's spiritual laws are continually troubled. They never rise to the level of abundance. They have no peace because various swords consume them.

STORY: It was after dark when my missionary team arrived in the remote agricultural village of Amuzedevi in the Volta Region of Ghana, Africa. We were deep in the jungle and many of the villagers had never seen Caucasians.

For 160 years, the villagers practiced paganism from generation to generation under the dominance of witchdoctors that ruled the spiritual atmosphere. However, in ninety minutes of preaching the Gospel, the entire village, including the king, queen mother, elders, witchdoctors, and fetich doctors all received Jesus Christ as their Lord and Savior. Only God could produce this miracle by the power of the Holy Spirit.

They were blessed with an abundance of life. Yet...I saw no toys, cars, electricity, cell phones, watches, newspapers—nothing of our modern amenities. However, God met everyone's needs in health, peace, happiness, food, shelter, and clothes. He blessed their crops, gave them safety, and healed them.

In the simplicity of their lives, God blessed them. Obedience to His Word worked for them just as well as it does in the complexity of any modern society.

★★★

> "Then Jesus said to them, 'Beware, and be on your guard against every form of greed; for not even when one has an abundance does his life consist of his possessions.'" (Luke 12:15)

Your needs are defined according to the sphere of life in which you dwell. Within that sphere, God abundantly supplies all your needs by obedience to His spiritual laws. In this regard, His spiritual laws work *for* you, not *against* you.

The Spiritual Law of Sowing and Reaping is a neutral law. It produces according to whatever is sown. Obedience reaps blessings. Disobedience reaps penalties. It is that simple.

The Spiritual Law of Sowing and Reaping

The Spiritual Law of the Implied Reverse joins to the **Law of Sowing and Reaping**. This means that every spiritual law has a reverse implied outcome. Paul explains these two laws in the following Scripture:

> "Now this I say, he who sows sparingly will reap sparingly, and he who sows bountifully will reap bountifully." *(2 Corinthians 2:6)*

If reoccurring troubles constantly surface, somewhere a sword is active. It is wise, therefore, to ask Jesus which laws have been violated, either by ignorance or deliberate action. What things were or are being sown that prevent total victory?

STORY: An assistant pastor along with several members of the church rallied against their senior pastor. Years later, the assistant pastor started his own church. Every time his church reached three hundred members a schism developed and the congregation split. This event kept repeating itself and soon the pattern was predictable. The pastor sought the Lord with fasting and prayer and asked why his church kept splitting at three hundred members.

The Lord showed him that when he was an assistant pastor, he along with multiple members of the congregation rallied against his senior pastor when the church had three hundred members. In the mind of those who opposed the senior pastor, their reasons were justified. According to their opinion, the senior pastor was wrong. But then again, was he?

This calls to mind **The Spiritual Law of Dignitary Authority**. Those whom the Lord divinely appoints to a position are "first" God's servants before they are the servants of any person. In this regard, no one has the authority to touch God's anointed leaders and stand against them. If His servants err, God deals with them directly.

The Spiritual Laws of Sowing and Reaping instantly came into play against the assistant pastor along with those who aligned with him. A sword was drawn against them. But, like the Chinese Bamboo that lay dormant for years, it stayed hidden until due time.

In this case, the sword against the pastor's ministry was not evident until years later when he had his own church. It cut precisely to the

The Spiritual Law of Sowing and Reaping

violation. Just as he split his pastor's church, he experienced repetitive splits in his church.

He had no idea that a sword was set against him. Consequently, his ministry was plagued with the same seeds he sowed against his senior pastor.

Realizing his demise, he confessed his sin to God. He then called his former senior pastor, confessed his sin to him, and asked for forgiveness. After *years* of turmoil and pain, the sword was removed. But of course, the pattern of church splits left many wounded Christians.

The sword was not limited to just the assistant pastor. It included those who aligned with him. Just as they troubled the Lord's house, their homes were troubled. And like the assistant pastor that did not realize the sword's *cause-and-effect*, likely those who aligned with him did not correlate the sword's penalty as it cut against their home. Defeat and strife would reign in their lives and even their children's lives to the third and fourth generation.

This brings up the subject concerning *the government of sin*. The collateral damage of sin often continues after the sword is removed. Even though the sin is forgiven, the wounds, pain, memories, and consequences do not necessarily disappear. There are after-effects that linger and sometimes are never forgotten.

After the sword was removed from the assistant pastor, his church began growing. It moved beyond three hundred people. And today is a thriving congregation in the multiple thousands of members.

***

> According to God's spiritual laws, violations
> of His moral and ethical laws
> automatically activate the sword.

In hindsight, several moral and ethical laws were violated that sent the sword against the assistant pastor.

The Spiritual Law of Sowing and Reaping

"These are six things the Lord hates; indeed seven that are repulsive to Him. 17 A proud look [the attitude that makes one overestimate oneself and discount others], a lying tongue and hands that shed innocent blood, 18 a heart that creates wicked plans, feet that run swiftly to evil, 19 a false witness who breathes out lies [even half-truths] and one who spreads discord among brothers." (Proverbs 6:16-19, The Amplified Bible. Square brackets added by author for clarity.)

The assistant pastor violated six of the seven sins that God lists as abominations:

(1) *"A proud look."* In his self-righteous pride as a champion of truth, he rallied against his senior pastor instead of praying for him and letting God render the judgment.

(2) *"A lying tongue."* The senior pastor's words were taken out of context and falsely presented. This conveniently served the spirit of sedition.

(3) *"A heart that creates wicked plans."* The malcontents who were infected with a seditious spirit, aligned with the assistant pastor and stood against the senior pastor. The entire group was rebellious and divisive. Everyone was infected with the spirit of rebellion.

(4) *"Feet that run swiftly to evil."* The assistant pastor rallied against his senior pastor. As a result, many people were wounded who were innocent of any wrongdoing.

(5) *"A false witness who breathes out lies."* There were half-truths, distorted words, and out of context statements. Like Satan, who is the accuser of the brethren, the assistant pastor sanctioned various lies in order to bolster the force of his sedition.

(6) *"One who spreads discord among brothers."* Using his trusted position, the assistant pastor troubled the Lord's house and unsettled the faith of many—a sin that carries serious repercussions.

When the assistant pastor violated God's moral and ethical laws, swords instantly activated against him along with those who participated in the rebellion.

The Spiritual Law of Sowing and Reaping

Blinded By Self-Justification

The sins of some are obvious by appearance; others are more subtle. Self-serving rationale is always used to justify sin. Regardless of the reasons, be it ignorance, confusion, or misunderstanding, the penalty of the sword does not change. It is mercilessly unbiased.

In the true story of the assistant pastor, he did not know he violated spiritual laws that sent swords against the future of his own ministry. Even worse, it took years before he understood the correlation between the swords and the outcome. Meanwhile, he repetitively experienced the same agony that he caused his senior pastor. Thankfully, the assistant pastor humbled himself and sought the Lord. If he had not, his ministry would have remained *mysteriously* troubled, burned out, and likely dismantled.

The Spiritual Law of the Seed

The Lord stands watch over His Word to perform it, EVERY SINGLE TIME; ALL THE TIME; EVERY SINGLE WORD; IN EVERY SINGLE DETAIL.

> *"Then said the Lord to me, you have seen well, for I am alert and active, watching over My Word to perform it."* (The Amplified Bible. Jeremiah 1:12)

The Spiritual Law of the Seed states that all things *must* produce after their kind (Genesis 1:11). There is no variance to this law.

The seed type defines the harvest type. Every seed must produce. Righteous seeds produce a righteous harvest and blessing. Unrighteous seeds produce an unrighteous harvest and penalty.

People are known by their fruit (Matthew 7:15-20). Those who sow discord, dissention, strife, and accusation *will* suffer the same seeds in their life. This law cannot be broken. Consequently, the *instant* unrighteous seed is sown, the sword is unsheathed and the penalty comes into play. And just as righteous seeds are sown, the process of blessings immediately begins as well.

Those who sow seeds according to the fruits of the Holy Spirit assure themselves great peace in their lives.

The Spiritual Law of Sowing and Reaping

Seeds, whatever their kind, be they good or bad, always bear an abundance of more than itself.

According to **The Spiritual Law of Manifold Returns**, a seed always produces an abundance of more than itself. A single seed produces many seeds. One apple seed produces a tree bearing many apples. Accordingly, seeds, whatever their kind, be they good or bad, always bear an abundance of more than itself. We see this law described in righteous sowing. But the same law produces the same effect in unrighteous sowing.

> *"Give, [sow] and it will be given [back] to you. They [your actions of sowing] will pour into your lap a good measure– pressed down, shaken together, and running over. For by your standard of measure [according to the measure of sowing] it will be measured [back] to you in return."* (Luke 6:38. Square brackets added by author for clarity.)

Exactly like the seeds of darkness, seeds of righteousness always produce an abundance. Therefore, it is important that we carefully consider our words and actions. They define the type of seed we sow and the harvest that follows.

God's Kingdom produces a harvest of continual abundance. There is no death or poverty in His Kingdom. Death and poverty are *outside* of His Kingdom. Conversely, God desires increase in every dimension of life for His children. His **Spiritual Law of Manifold Returns** guarantees an *increase* by the harvest of righteousness!

Equally so, when seeds of unrighteousness are sown, this law produces a sword of vengeance against those who sow evil. It returns in manifold strength.

Good or bad, every seed produces a harvest.

The Offset of One Against the Other

Regardless of our righteous standing in salvation, if seeds of unrighteousness are sown, the sword is activated. Remember: every seed

The Spiritual Law of Sowing and Reaping

produces a manifold return. Thus, our lives can be victorious in some areas and frustrated in other areas. It is important, therefore, to bring everything before the Lord. By His Spirit, every sword can be identified. And by confession and repentance, it can be removed.

Even though the assistant pastor had limited measures of success, his church kept splitting. He could never rise above the limit of the sword. The sword remained active in his ministry until he confessed his sin to both God and man. He then had to make the required restitution.

Our Father's spiritual laws are unbiased. They reflect His unbiased righteousness and unchanging character. Whenever we violate His Word, the seed we plant *must bear a manifold return*. Satan knows this! If he can cause people to sin, it brings God's sword against them and halts their progress.

With great joy, the spiritual laws of sowing and reaping work to our advantage. Paul explained the blessings of this spiritual law to the Corinthian church. It is based on **The Spiritual Law of Manifold Returns** in tandem with **The Spiritual Law of Sowing and Reaping.** I call this passage, "The Infinity Blessing":

> *"Each one must do just as he has purposed in his heart, not grudgingly or under compulsion, for God loves a cheerful giver. 8 And God is able to make all grace abound to you, so that always having all sufficiency in everything, you may have an abundance for every good deed; 9 as it is written, 'He scattered abroad, He gave to the poor, his righteousness endures forever.' 10 Now He who supplies seed to the sower and bread for food will supply and multiply your seed for sowing and increase the harvest of your righteousness; 11 you will be enriched in everything for all liberality, which through us is producing thanksgiving to God."*
> (2 Corinthians 9:7-11)

> *"Give, and you will receive. Your gift will return to you in full—pressed down, shaken together to make room for more, running over, and poured into your lap. The amount you give will determine the amount you get back."* (Luke 6:38. The New Living Translation)

The Spiritual Law of Sowing and Reaping

The Spiritual Law of the Implied Reverse is equally potent when violated. Nothing sown means a harvest of nothing when needs arise. This is the spirit of poverty that comes through disobedience. Therefore, remember the sober warning of Romans 13:4, where it says:

> *"For it* [authority] *is a minister of God to you for good. But if you do what is evil, be afraid; for it* [authority] *does not bear the sword for nothing; for it* [authority] *is a minister of God, an avenger who brings wrath on the one who practices evil."* (Square brackets added by author for clarity.)

For this reason, the beginning of *wisdom* is to fear the Lord. He is His Word and His Word is Him. They are indivisible. He will always do what He said. Therefore, walk circumspectly by considering the outcome of your actions according to the seeds planted.

The seeds that a fool sows are difficult for him to understand its *cause-and-effect*. When the sword cuts, he has no idea why or for what reason.

> *"The fear of the Lord, is the beginning of wisdom, and the knowledge of the Holy One is understanding."* (Proverbs 9:10)

Chapter Four
The Spiritual Laws of Mercy, Grace, and the Government of Sin

"The sins of some men are quite evident. Going on before them to judgment, for others their sins follow after. 25 Likewise also, deeds that are good are quite evident, and those which are otherwise cannot be concealed." (1 Timothy 5:25)

God's character, which is love, is unchangeable. From His love flows mercy, and from His mercy flows grace, and from His grace flows faith—the faith He gives that enables us to believe His every Word (Ephesians 2:8) which produces blessings in our lives.

Our confidence in God's love releases our faith for action. Because we know He loves us, we have a confident hope that yields an absolute return. But if there is no hope, our faith cannot work. Love empowers hope; hope empowers faith.

> *"But now faith, hope, and love abide these three, but the greatest of these is love." (1 Corinthians 13:13)*

The Bible is replete with verses that testify of God's faithfulness, compassion, mercy, grace, steadfast patience, and unwavering love. However, in all of these virtues, we must understand *the requirements of His truth* that perfectly complement His character.

The Spiritual Laws of Mercy, Grace, and the Government of Sin

Spiritually immature Christians, including people in the secular world, are generally ignorant about God's love. Presumptuously, they misapply the truth of His love and use it as a hall-pass for their sin.

The metro-style gay and lesbian churches are one such example. By first eliminating the context of *truth* that define the righteousness of our Father, they misapply His love as it serves them according to their own lusts. Consequently, their concept of God's love has no truth in it. They assume God accepts and endorses their homosexual lifestyles because they have love one for another. In church, they sing the same songs of worship, receive Holy Communion, weep at His altars, and say the same prayers. Meanwhile, God deems their lifestyles as an abomination to Him.

> **Many Christians wonder why their lives cannot rise to a higher level. They have no idea that they are living under the penalty of God's sword.**

Since we are saved by grace and not by works, immature Christians assume that sin has little or no penalty. According to their logic, God's love covers us and we are immune to any reprisals of the sword. Ha! Satan takes no prisoners—he steals, kills, and destroys everything.

The drug addict shooting poison into his veins claims that God loves him just as he is. And that is true. But truth demands that he repents.

The alcoholic gulping poison into his body claims that God loves him just as he is. And that is true. But truth demands that he repents.

The morbidly obese person shoveling food down his throat claims that God loves him just as he is. And that is true. But truth demands that he repents.

Even though God loves them, when they violate **The Spiritual Law of Stewardship,** they incur a sword against their health. Any of them can die in their sin while God loves them.

The Spiritual Laws of Mercy, Grace, and the Government of Sin

In the church of Corinth, Paul lists ten lifestyles for which those who practice them will not inherit God's Kingdom. And remember, he is speaking this to Christians.

> *"Do you not know that the wicked will not inherit the Kingdom of God? Do not be deceived: neither the sexually immoral nor idolaters nor adulterers nor male prostitutes nor homosexual offenders 10 nor thieves nor greedy nor drunkards nor swindlers will inherit the Kingdom of God."* (1 Corinthians 6:9-10)

(1) Wicked lifestyles.
(2) Sexually immoral lifestyles.
(3) Idolatrous lifestyles.
(4) Adulterous lifestyles.
(5) Prostitution lifestyles.
(6) Homosexual lifestyles.
(7) Thievery lifestyles.
(8) Greedy lifestyles.
(9) Drunkard (alcoholic) lifestyles.
(10) Swindling lifestyles.

Many Christians live under the penalty of the sword(s) and consequently they cannot rise above their challenges. They struggle repetitively with the same issues and do not know why they cannot overcome. Their forward progress is blocked by violations of the spiritual laws. Even worse, their families are plagued with bewildering and bizarre attacks.

These are symptoms of an active sword somewhere in their life. God loves them and wants them delivered. For that reason, they must seek Him to find out why the sword has power against them. Once the Lord shows them the sword, it can be removed by repentance.

Just as any natural law, such as gravity, the sword of God's spiritual laws is unbiased. His spiritual laws do not grant favors or exceptions. Consequently, God's great love does not offset the working of His spiritual laws.

The Spiritual Laws of Mercy, Grace, and the Government of Sin

He loves those who are compliant as much as those who are in violation. But, we must understand that His love does not exempt us from His spiritual laws. It is these very laws that produce our blessings by obedience, or, a sword by disobedience.

For example, **The Spiritual Law of Moral Duty** requires that a husband respects his wife as the physically weaker vessel. If he mistreats her, an immediate sword is brought against him. His prayers will be hindered or altogether cut off. Heaven is closed to him as he appeals to God for various needs.

> *"You husbands in the same way, live with your wives in an understanding way, as with someone* [physically] *weaker, since she is a woman, and show her honor as a fellow heir of the grace of life, so that your prayers will not be hindered." (1 Peter 3:7. Square brackets added by author for clarity.)*

In marriage, **The Spiritual Law of Moral Duty** requires that each spouse fulfill their marital duty toward one another in sexual intimacy. If this is violated, Satan seizes the opportunity and sends in his agents of adultery. Therefore, God prohibits the husband and wife from withholding their bodies from each other. Nor is it permissible to manipulate one another by using intimacy to coerce their spouse into compliance.

> *"The wife does not have authority over her body, but the husband does, and likewise also the husband does not have authority over his own body, but the wife does. 5 Stop depriving one another, except by agreement for time, so that you may devote yourselves to prayer, and come together again so that Satan will not tempt you because of your lack of self-control." (1 Corinthians 7:4-5)*

Every situation requires a righteous response. In this regard, moral duty extends itself in a much broader sense. In various states, for example, if a motorist comes upon an auto accident, there are laws that require motorists to stop and render aid. Failure to do so is a criminal violation.

The Spiritual Laws of Mercy, Grace, and the Government of Sin

Using the same moral truth, Jesus tells the parable of the Good Samaritan who helped a man that was beaten by robbers and left to die. The Samaritan picked up the man, treated his wounds, and paid for the man's lodging so he could rest and recover (Luke 10:30-37).

The Spiritual Law of Moral Duty is defined in Scripture where James says:

> *"Therefore, to one who knows the right thing to do and does not do it, to him, it is sin."* (James 4:17)

Based on the above Scripture, acts of *omission* can be sin just as acts of *commission* can be sin. The one who knows to do good and does it not, is sinning. For example, *ignoring* the poor and needy when it is clearly within one's power to help, sets a sword in motion. We saw this in the parable of the rich man and Lazarus (Luke 16:19-31).

> *"He who shuts his ear to the cry of the poor will also cry himself and not be answered".* (Proverbs 21:13)

In this case, when **The Spiritual Law of Moral Duty** is violated, the sword comes into play according to **The Spiritual Law of Manifold Returns**.

This deserves a note of wisdom: many imposters, posing as beggars, exploit people's compassion. They are professional hucksters. Therefore, be led by the Holy Spirit when considering what to give. Do not be compelled by false condemnation when passing by such scammers.

You May Be Surprised

Related to **The Spiritual Law of the Canopy,** Paul applied his Apostolic authority. (This is explained in Part II.) The enemy is an ever constant, relentless, presence set against us. The moment we violate God's spiritual laws, it creates an opening and he comes rushing in.

> *"Whoever digs a pit may fall into it; whoever breaks through a wall may be bitten by a snake."* (Ecclesiastes 10:8. New International Version.)

The Spiritual Laws of Mercy, Grace, and the Government of Sin

In the above verse, the person who metaphorically digs a pit will be victim to his own actions. The trap he set for others will be the trap he sets for himself. And the person who steps out from their divine covering is instantly vulnerable to the enemy.

Those that aligned with the assistant pastor's deceit removed themselves from God's divine protection. By violating **The Spiritual Law of the Canopy,** they dangerously exposed themselves to the enemy.

> *"He who* [willfully] *separates himself seeks his own desire, he quarrels against all sound wisdom."* (Proverbs 18:1. Square brackets added by author for clarity.

The man whom Paul turned over to Satan, a "Christian man" by the way, lived in sin and refused to repent. Accordingly, Paul removed the man's protective canopy, which, up to that point, remained in place while the Lord gave him time to repent. But, he refused to turn from his sin. Consequently, with the canopy removed, the Destroyer rushed in and attacked his body.

The sword constructively worked for repentance. In Paul's second letter to the Corinthians, he instructed the church to restore him.

> *"Now if anyone has caused grief, he has not grieved me but all of you—to some degree, not to overstate it. 6 The punishment imposed on him by the majority is sufficient for him. 7 So instead, you ought to forgive and comfort him, so that he will not be overwhelmed by excessive sorrow."* (2 Corinthians 2:5-7)

Because of ignorance and presumption regarding God's grace, some Christians find it conflicting that any *Believer* could be turned over to *Satan* for the destruction of their flesh. They think such judgment could never happen because we are protected by Jesus. This is because they view God's mercy through their personal sense of justice rather than through His immutable Word.

By such presumption, they think they can annul, rebuke, or invalidate righteous edicts such as Paul's authority to do what he did, or when God issues a prophetic warning through His servants.

The Spiritual Laws of Mercy, Grace, and the Government of Sin

> **When the sword of God's Word is levied against a Christian, the first thing immature Christians do is rebuke Satan's works when in fact it is not Satan, but God.**

If this scenario happened today, immature Christians would gather an entourage of like-minded naïve Christians. Under **The Spiritual Law of Agreement**, they would denounce all words of judgment. Vainly, they would issue decrees with rebukes against such words as if standing in the authority of Jesus and commanding the forces of darkness to cease.

They do not realize it is God's sword they are trying to annul. Thinking that their words carry power, they presumptuously walk in false authority. Being soul-driven rather than being led by the Holy Spirit, their words are a waste of breath. In their fallacious logic, they reason that:

1. We are no longer under the curse. Therefore, anyone speaking such declarations speak by the spirit of witchcraft.

2. As Christians, it is unloving to decree such an edict. Therefore, it cannot be from the Lord.

3. Because we are under grace, Paul had no authority from God to make such judgment.

4. We have the power to rebuke and nullify such unrighteous decrees.

5. Such decrees are inconsistent with God's character of love.

6. A covenant keeping God would not hand His children over to Satan.

The Spiritual Laws of Mercy, Grace, and the Government of Sin

7. God says He will never forsake us, therefore this could not be from the Lord.

Such platitudes race through the minds of naïve untaught and spiritually immature Christians.

Especially today, when God's sword comes against a Christian, the first thing immature Christians do is rebuke Satan's works. In fact, it is not Satan, but God's spiritual laws that levies the sword! Consequently, no Christian has the power to rebuke the truth or stop God's sword, which they mistakenly presume to be the work of darkness.

No one is exempt from God's spiritual laws. The only saving grace, (depending on the offense), is the degree to which God holds back the Destroyer as an act of "measured mercy". But know for certain, the sword is God's avenger against those who practice evil. It works every time. It is precise, exact, and applied according to the offense.

Stumbling Sins verses Lifestyle Sins

Does a single event of sin draw a lesser penalty than lifestyle sins? Let us consider King David's life to answer that question. When David committed adultery with Bathsheba, it was a single event. It was not an affair. It was a stumbling sin, not a lifestyle sin.

After David impregnated Bathsheba, he arranged for Bathsheba's husband, Uriah, to be killed in battle in order to hide David's adulterous shame.

According to Jewish law, there was no acceptable sacrifice for murder or adultery. The penalty was death. Nonetheless, God forgave David of both sins. However, the government of David's sin drew a sword that immediately went into effect.

Based on these two acts of sin, murder and adultery, the sword would never depart from David's immediate house. Even though God forgave him, and even though God loved him, his household was troubled from that point forward.

The Spiritual Laws of Mercy, Grace, and the Government of Sin

"Now therefore, the sword shall never depart from your house, because you have despised Me and have taken the wife of Uriah the Hittite [a Gentile woman] to be your wife. 11 Thus says the Lord, 'Behold, I will raise up evil against you from your own household; I will even take your wives before your eyes and give them to your companion, and he will lie with your wives in broad daylight. 12 Indeed you did it in secret, but I will do this thing before all Israel, and under the sun." (2 Samuel 12:10-12. Square brackets added by author for clarity.)

Some might argue that David was not under the dispensation of grace as we are today. Erroneously, many use the "Grace Credit Card Theory" to assuage their sense of guilt.

Even though we are under grace by salvation, such grace does not negate violations of God's *spiritual laws*. For example, **The Spiritual Law of Sowing and Reaping** that applied to David also applies today. It is immutable. It works every single time.

STORY: A man whom I regarded as a truthful person testified as a witness in court for the defense in one of my criminal cases. When he was asked a certain question by the prosecution, he knew the answer would be condemning evidence against the defendant who was his friend.

He took a calculated risk and lied under oath. Unfortunately, his lie was exposed by taped evidence shown in the court. The judge held him in contempt and he spent ten days in jail. He lost a third of his wages that month, incurred a criminal record for perjury, was humiliated in the newspapers, and endured open shame for his actions.

God forgave him for lying, a singular event, but the government of his sin continued as he endured public disgrace.

✶✶✶

A lifestyle sin is something repetitively and continually practiced without repentance. This means there is little or no resistance against it. Addiction of any kind, for example, is a sword for refusing to repent.

The Spiritual Laws of Mercy, Grace, and the Government of Sin

Without repentance, the sword's power is unstoppable. God alone sets the limits of its judgments. Further, the only person who can stop the sword is the person who activated it. And the only way to do that is through confession of the sin, repentance, and restoration.

STORY: As a police officer, I had frequent encounters with a violent young man in his late twenties. Every time I arrested him, he had be tased into compliance and spoke threats of killing me.

On one occasion while booking him into jail, he started escalating with threats. He said he knew where I like to fish and threatened to shoot me with his rifle from a great distance away.

I looked at him and said, "Alex, if you live by the sword, by the sword you will die." He exploded into rage, charged at me with swinging fists, and was again tased into submission.

A few months later while I was on patrol, my police radio picked up conversations between officers from a nearby jurisdiction. They reported a knife fight and mentioned Alex's name as one of the suspects. In the scuffle, Alex was also stabbed.

To hide from the police, he fled the premises and ran out of the house onto the open prairie and hid in the dark of the night. He was found several weeks later when someone stumbled upon his body. After losing too much blood, he weakened, fell, and died. When they found him, he was half-eaten by the coyotes.

Little did I realize, I spoke a prophetic warning to him about his violent credo. And while he issued words of murder against my life, he had no idea that he drew the sword against himself.

★★★

Equally as powerful are the blessings of obedience. In joy, God celebrates over us. It is His good pleasure to give us the treasures of His Kingdom! He is not withholding them. He only asks for our obedience in order to release them!

The Spiritual Laws of Mercy, Grace, and the Government of Sin

Nothing can undo God's Word! His truth is not affected by anyone's opinion or personal belief. Useless declarations, presented as spiritual authority that are uttered against His edicts, amount to nothing more than futility. Those speaking raucous words of binding and loosening, or rebuking and denouncing, foolishly think they possess God's Kingdom Authority. In fact, they walk in vain imaginations.

Truth is unassailable by declarations of binding and loosening disguised as the authority of God's Word.

STORY: A young man sat at the back of my church with a few of his friends. Suddenly, in the middle of my message, the Lord gave me a prophetic word for him. I stopped, looked at him, addressed him by name and said, "If you don't stop doing what you are doing right now, you'll be getting your mail in a different location for a long time."

Some might define this as speaking a curse over his life. Others saw it as a declaration of his future. In any case, he was in a lifestyle sin. God warned him in order to save him from a consequence of bitter regret. Unfortunately, he didn't listen.

A month later he was arrested by federal DEA agents for dealing heavy drugs and was subsequently sent to federal prison for ten years. God forgave him and he showed genuine repentance. But the sword remains until his sentence is served.

The government of his sin carried bitter regret. For ten years, he could not be an interactive father with his son. For ten years, he was absent from his family's joys and tribulations in life.

Finishing his prison sentence is part of the sword, but the other part is losing things he can never regain. It was a heavy price to pay. Had he listened to the Word of Knowledge and the Word of Wisdom, he could have avoided a tragedy that took a third of his life.

★★★

The Spiritual Laws of Mercy, Grace, and the Government of Sin

STORY: A middle-aged obese woman in church was caught up in the spirit of offense when the pastor gave her a confirming prophetic word—a word which she said the Lord had already spoken to her.

The pastor said to her, "There is something related to your health that God has been speaking to you for which you are procrastinating."

She immediately agreed. She affirmed she had been putting off exercising—something the Lord spoke to her that was related to her morbid obesity from which she struggled most of her life.

Being divorced from two previous husbands, she wanted to marry again. However, her physical appearance made her considerably less attractive. Had she received the Word and not despised the prophetic utterance, it would have been the turning point in her life.

In the previous few years, she asked the pastor to help her with pursuits in ministry. He told her there would be instances when she needed to square with the truth; that at times it might be confronting; and that life was not always pleasant when breaking through strongholds. Despite these realities, she wanted the pastor's help.

On the occasion in question, when the pastor gave her the prophetic word, she was immediately offended. What she didn't recognize was the critical spirit that Satan was cultivating in her. He was setting her up for an opportune moment. Consequently, She resented the message and went after the messenger—the pastor—thus violating **The Spiritual Law of Dignitary Authority** where God says:

> "Do not touch My anointed one, and do My prophets no harm."
> (1 Chronicles 16:22)

> "He who receives you, receives Me, and he who receives Me receives Him who sent Me. He who receives a prophet in the name of a prophet shall receive a prophet's reward, and he who receives a righteous man in the name of a righteous man shall receive a righteous man's reward." (Matthew 10:40-41)

The Spiritual Laws of Mercy, Grace, and the Government of Sin

Exactly as the above verse states, this spiritual law is based on **The Law of Vicarious Transfer**. When God sends His servants (anyone whom He chooses) to speak a message, it is as if the Lord spoke it in person (Matthew 10:41-42). Consequently, He warns people not to violate His servants.

This spiritual law is frequently ignored throughout the Bible which often resulted in the death or abuse of God's messengers and harsh judgment to the perpetrator.

As the woman mused on the word given to her, a word she did not like, Satan worked on her. The stronghold of her obesity was worsening. She turned against the pastor and opened herself to a satanically inspired influence. Anger grew within her and she twisted God's prophetic word and used it as a false accusation against her pastor.

The pastor ultimately confronted her about harboring the spirit of offense. He told her that if she didn't get it under control, Satan would use it to destroy her.

Instead of humbly receiving the prophetic word, she retaliated with reckless actions. She secretly campaigned throughout the church looking for weak Christians to join her and accused the pastor of various things. Using half-truths and out of context claims, she recruited anyone that was foolish enough to get entangled in her satanic lies.

In previous months, the woman was heard bragging that her employment trained her how to lie in order to increase her sales in the cell phone business. Sadly, she used the same skill in troubling the Lord's house.

Under the pretense of seeking godly counsel, she viciously gossiped about the pastor while stirring up strife and division among members of the church. She rounded up six other people who foolishly aligned with her. Little did she know, she set the sword against the future of her ministry, household, and the issue of her obesity. As for the other six people, the sword levied itself against them as well:

The Spiritual Laws of Mercy, Grace, and the Government of Sin

(1) One senior single woman left the church. She wandered about and did not know where to go for fellowship. As she troubled the Lord's house, her house was troubled as well. Her daughter fought sudden intense bouts of life-threatening alcoholism. This necessitated a series of 500-mile drives back and forth to help her daughter. With no spiritual covering, the wandering Christian found herself fighting the battles alone. She also endured financial issues and eventually settled in a church very mismatched with her faith. Later she admitted deep regret for allowing herself to get involved with the obese woman. But, the sword remains until she confesses her sin against God's house.

(2) A husband and wife's house was troubled as well. A daughter from his former marriage distanced herself even further from him. When they left the church that God assigned to them, the wife settled in another church mismatched with her faith. Wandering and discouraged, the husband decided to go nowhere but stayed at home. Their spiritual agreement as a household of faith was divided. Consequently, the sword remains until the anger and unforgiveness she harbors is confessed before the Lord.

(3) A mother and daughter team wandered about as well. The husband's chronic physical health issues took a turn for the worse and he ended up in the hospital. The truth is, this was their pattern lifestyle of church hopping under the self-acclaimed pretense of being highly spiritual and sensitive to the Holy Spirit. Other swords were already present in their lives.

(4) Another single woman experienced troubling issues in her house with her daughter who was fighting severe demonic issues. The woman joined a church that was very mismatched with her faith. Unlike the others, she reconciled with her former pastor but never completed the process. She is now in a position outside of the perfect will of God. She too was remorseful about getting involved with the obese woman.

(5) The ringleader, the obese woman, lost her job, had to move to a different city for employment, left her house which she had bought only a few years before, and remains financially stressed.

The Spiritual Laws of Mercy, Grace, and the Government of Sin

Her household is fractured with issues and complications. Spiritually, she is a mess. And the sword remains until she confesses her sin against God's house.

The Way You Go Out, Is The Way You Go In

When God transitions His children from one thing into another, the fruits of the Holy Spirit are clearly manifest in the works of His wisdom:

> *"But the wisdom from above is first pure* [morally and spiritually undefiled], *then peace-loving* [courteous, considerate], *gentle, reasonable* [and willing to listen], *full of compassion and good fruits. It is unwavering, without* [self-righteous] *hypocrisy* [and self-serving guile]." (James 3:17. The Amplified Bible. Square brackets added by author for clarity.)

The above verse follows **The Spiritual Law of Continuity**. Continuity means: an unbroken consistent operation without contradiction. In other words, God's leads by unbroken continuous righteousness which always bears the Fruit of the Holy Spirit in every aspect through all the transitions.

When people leave in pride, anger, offense, arrogance, or in any manner of unrighteousness, they enter the next thing the same way. This is a spiritual law. Furthermore, pride, anger, and offense is ALWAYS justified by self-serving rational. Therefore, in all decisions of life, *always* leave and enter according to God's righteousness.

According to **The Spiritual Law of Continuity**, God always leads a person by four resolute principles:

From grace to grace: (John 1:16).
From strength to strength: (Psalm 84:7)
From faith to faith: (Romans 1:17)
From glory to glory: (2 Corinthians 3:18)

When our Father *promotes* us from one phase into the other, we move from grace to grace: from one level of His divine impartation

The Spiritual Laws of Mercy, Grace, and the Government of Sin

an increasing in grace to the next level. Grace, in this sense means a divinely imparted ability to perform.

During the same process, He enlarges our strength by adding more strength. Then He gives a divine operations of faith, added to the faith we already possess in order to finish our advancement from one level of glory into the next level of glory.

Referring again to the obese woman's roundup of the six weak Christians (the five women and one man) that followed her, **The Spiritual Law of Agreement** drew them together by **The Spiritual Law of Alignment**. And by **The Spiritual Law of Transfer** they were given over to a common spirit.

Look at the fruits that came out of their decisions: wandering from church to church, mismatched context, unsettled in faith, unresolved anger, schism, implosion, troubled households, without continuity, financial issues, troubled children, scattered, isolation, and disenfranchised from one another. Nothing in their decision met the standard of God's divine wisdom as defined by James. They were completely absent of the fruit of the Holy Spirit.

They were blind to Satan's ploy as he skillfully moved among them. He used them as agents of strife and then tossed them to the junkpile of discarded souls. Immediately after he was finished with them, they dispersed one from the other and in some cases turned against each other. Today, according to **The Spiritual Law of Pairing** they remain mismatched in the context of their faith and greatly stifled in their spiritual rate of growth.

Of the seven deadly sins listed in Proverbs 6:16-19, the obese woman broke five of them along with several other Scriptures.

The Law of Spiritual Alignment binds people in the common influence of spiritual agreement, either to the good or the bad.

The Spiritual Laws of Mercy, Grace, and the Government of Sin

In her anger and reckless actions against the Lord's house, she spread her seditious spirit and troubled the faith of many. Grievous swords remain in her life.

The pastor's warning that was given to her in the Spirit, was not the utterance of a curse as she claimed. Rather, it was God's mercy to turn her from further damage against herself and others. Instead, she distorted the Word, accused it, and presented herself as a victim. The group she gathered then aligned with her darkness. According to **The Spiritual Law of Alignment,** the sword was set into motion against their lives as well.

After recklessly violating several spiritual laws, the woman crossed the "tipping point". The penalty of the sword moved into action. The damage she imposed against her life is now incalculable. Like the Chinese Bamboo that lies dormant for five years and then suddenly surged in growth, the sword will be evident in its season in multiple areas of her life.

"If" she can ever recognize the action of the sword, she will have two choices: Without the repentance required of her, she will live an *adjusted life* to the sword's action, or, she will seek the Lord for forgiveness as well as those she harmed. Only by repentance through humility can the sword be removed.

Without repentance, the sword remains perpetually active in her life. And as long as it does, she and those who aligned with her will never see the potential that God called them to achieve. The consequential government of their actions will frustrate their progress in life. Not in all areas, but in key areas specific to their offense. The sword she incurred holds her in limitation as a point of continual obstruction against greatness. This is exactly what happened to the assistant pastor who split his pastor's church. By God's grace, however, he repented and came into his greatness.

> "For if we go on sinning willfully after receiving the knowledge of the truth, there no longer remains a sacrifice for our sins, 27 but a terrifying expectation of judgment and the fury of a fire which will consume the adversaries." *(Hebrews 10:26-27)*

The Spiritual Laws of Mercy, Grace, and the Government of Sin

The Law of Spiritual Alignment yokes people together. This is a neutral law that depends on what is sown. For example, Korah, Dathan, and Abiram arrogantly accused Moses of his decisions in their journey through the desert—which, by the way, were God's decisions, not Moses'.

Unless intercepted, the spirit of self-justified offense is an aggressive *fast* gathering storm. This case was no different. In a short time among the three million Israelites, three men secretly gathered two hundred fifty leaders that spiritually aligned with each other. Ultimately, God judged them unto death for their mutinous ploy. (Numbers 16:1-32)

The Law of Spiritual Alignment is also a blessing. On the day of Pentecost, one hundred twenty people in the upper room were in one accord when the Holy Spirit came upon them with tongues of fire. Even following that event, the early church was powerfully aligned with each other, and everyone shared anything they had with those who lacked.

The Law of Spiritual Alignment is also seen among the Apostles where Jesus said:

> "The glory which You have given me I have given them, that they may be one, just as We are one." *(John 17:22)*

The potential of any spiritual alignment always comes with a sober warning which, in brief, is this: *carefully consider your affiliations*. Be led by the Holy Spirit and always scrutinize people's motive before you align with them. Do they stand square with truth and righteousness? Are there fruits of humility? Do they stand in Kingdom Authority? Do they honor God's spiritual leaders? Does what they do and say line up *exactly* with God's Word?

Hymenaeus and Philetus characterize this principle quite clearly:

> "But avoid worldly and empty chatter for it will lead to further ungodliness, 17 and their talk will spread like gangrene. Among them are Hymenaeus and Philetus, 18 men who have gone astray

The Spiritual Laws of Mercy, Grace, and the Government of Sin

from the truth...and they upset the faith of some." (2 Timothy 2:16-18b)

Except that *some* people spiritually aligned with them, Hymenaeus and Philetus could not upset anyone's faith.

The Apostle Paul, a man of great love and fatherly compassion, handed a "Christian" man over to Satan (1 Corinthians 5:5). While this is considered extreme discipline, the sword's vengeance is always proportionate to the offense.

In the Bible, Paul was the greatest revelator of salvation by faith. It is also to be noted that when certain "Christians" were handed over to Satan, it was <u>in this present age of GRACE</u>.

According to Scripture, the "Christian" whom Paul handed over to Satan was having sex with his father's wife. Maybe his father was deceased. Or, maybe they were separated. Perhaps he loved the woman and justified his actions on the merits of his emotions. We only have limited information about the situation. In any case, it was wrong. The man defiantly remained in the church and refused to repent. Because of his obstinance, he was turned over to Satan for the destruction of his flesh!

"Idealistic Christians" have a hard time reconciling their immature concepts of God's grace with His sword. Much to their surprise, God's grace is not a hall-pass that exempts anyone from the consequence of sin.

It is wise to remember that in this present age of GRACE, Ananias and Sapphira were judged unto death when they lied to the Holy Spirit (Acts 4:1-12). They showed no regard for His manifest glory proven by His signs and wonders. They sinned in the clear understanding of the truth.

Again, the sword cuts in exact proportion to the degree of the sin.

Regarding the morbidly obese woman that stirred up strife and troubled the faith of many in her church, consequential judgments are

The Spiritual Laws of Mercy, Grace, and the Government of Sin

activated against her life by the seeds she planted. She ignored the warnings God gave her and instead became an attacker.

This doesn't necessarily mean she will lose her salvation. However, episodic troubles will repetitively surge in specific areas of her life until she repents of her offense. If she fails to repent, her hopes for ministry will never be fulfilled. She will forever be learning, but never advancing or achieving. She will continually experience setbacks, flat-lines, and remain non-progressive. Everything she endeavors in ministry will be nothing more than lateral shifting, but never forward advancing. Her busy efforts will never produce increasing spiritual depth because God cannot trust her with a deeper anointing.

Despite her great efforts to move forward, her returns will be minuscule. In all likelihood, because of the sword's enigma and her disregard for Kingdom Authority, she will ultimately walk away from her calling and blame others for her demise. Eventually, she will lose all passion for serving Jesus. Ministry will only be a passing dream she once considered.

Whether by her innocence or ignorance, the sword remains in her life. It remains just as it did with the assistant pastor who violated his senior pastor's ministry. It is hidden like the Chinese Bamboo. In due season, it will reach full status.

She is the *only one* who can remove the sword. This requires humility, confessing her fault to all whom she troubled, the church, and even those she duped into alignment with her. This judgment also applies to those who joined her.

> "But to this one I will look, to him who is humble and contrite of spirit, and who trembles at My Word." *(Isaiah 66:2)*

Chapter Five
Removing the Sword

"God is loving, merciful, and compassionate. In the words of Jesus, He said, "I am the way the truth and the life; no one comes to the Father but through Me." John 14:6

Life flourishes within the design of God's Kingdom. Everything is based on knowing Him through the Holy Spirit's revelation and obedience to His Word. In combination, these make an unstoppable blessed life!

All functions of life and blessings are based on obedience to our Heavenly Father's spiritual laws. Because of His unchanging and unwavering righteousness, His blessings are guaranteed through obedience to His Word. If we do what He said to do, then He will do what He promised to do.

God's spiritual laws govern the natural realm at all times. For example, the earth travels at 67,000 mph around the sun in a counter-clockwise direction at 1037.69 mile per hour with a 23.4 degree tilt on its axis. It makes a full rotation every 23 hours, 56 minutes, and 4.0953 seconds.

Is our faith required for earth to maintain its orbital path? Obviously not. God's laws keep it in precise motion, speed, and timing.

Removing the Sword

In the same way, God does not require our faith for His spiritual laws to work. They are subject only to Him. In fact, most people are unaware that His spiritual laws even exist.

Being Blessed!

Jesus is the doorway of *truth*, the only access to an "abundant life". Life begins with Him! However, abundance is stifled when God's spiritual laws are violated. Conversely, when His spiritual laws are obeyed, abundance is released.

**The spiritual laws apply to all people at all times.
Faith is not required for them to work.**

The enemy has three objectives: to kill, steal, and destroy. To do his works, he must have license. He cannot arbitrarily destroy at will. Therefore, he seeks an open door—a violation of God's immutable Word. He does this through people's ignorance, confusion, offenses, self-styled independence, sin, self-justification, condemnation, and so forth. He studies a person, catalogues their weaknesses, and sets up the bait.

> "Simon, Simon, behold, Satan has demanded permission to sift you like wheat, 32 But I have prayed for you, Simon, that your faith will not fail. And when you have turned back, strengthen your brothers." *(Luke 22:31-32)*

> "My people are destroyed for lack of knowledge. Because you have rejected knowledge, I will also reject you from being My priest.[5] Since you have forgotten the law of your God, I will also forget your children." *(Hosea 4:6)*

> "For the wrath of God is revealed from Heaven against all ungodliness and unrighteousness of men who suppress the truth in unrighteousness." *(Romans 1:18)*

---

[5] "You also, as living stones, are being built up as a spiritual house for a holy priesthood to offer up spiritual scarifies to God through Jesus Christ. 1 Peter 2:5

Removing the Sword

Any violation of God's spiritual laws always produce a sword. There is no such thing as sin without a cost, or a violation without a sword.

In the same way, blessings are just as absolute when we obey God's spiritual laws. In fact, it is these very spiritual laws that ensure our blessings by obedience.

STORY: Edwin Cole, author of <u>Maximized Manhood</u>, told me the story of a pastor who *unknowingly* violated **The Spiritual Law of Alignment** in tandem with **The Spiritual Law of Pairing**.

Ed was a guest speaker at a church and the host pastor picked him up at the airport. The usual small talk ensued and the pastor mentioned how the church's tithes and offerings were noticeably down for some unknown reason. Ed asked about the leadership of the church, specifically the elders. One particular elder was in a financial situation because of his personal mismanagement. Wanting to protect the elder's reputation, the pastor loaned him a certain amount of money through the church. In so doing, the pastor unwittingly paired the church with the elder's sin by spiritual alignment. Ed told the pastor that he needed to bring the elder before the leadership of the church, correct him, and then admit the fault to the congregation. The pastor followed Ed's counsel. Within the same week, the tithes and offerings returned to normal levels.

Most people in the church had no idea that a sword was levied against the finances. They simply lost their passion to give. Because of the pastor's violation of the two spiritual laws, God's grace had lifted from the hearts of the congregation members.

✯✯✯

Is It A Curse or the Sword?

"So you, son of man: I have made you a watchman for the house of Israel; therefore you shall hear a word from My mouth and warn them for Me. 8 When I say to the wicked, 'O wicked man, you shall surely die!' and you do not speak to warn the wicked from his way, that wicked man shall die in his iniquity; but his blood I will require at your hand. 9 Nevertheless if you warn the wicked to turn from his way, and he does not turn from his way,

Removing the Sword

he shall die in his iniquity; but you have delivered your soul." (Ezekiel 33:7-9)

"Therefore you, O son of man, say to the children of your people: 'The righteousness of the righteous man shall not deliver him in the day of his transgression; as for the wickedness of the wicked, he shall not fall because of it in the day that he turns from his wickedness; nor shall the righteous be able to live because of his righteousness in the day that he sins.' 13 When I say to the righteous that he shall surely live, but he trusts in his own righteousness and commits iniquity, none of his righteous works shall be remembered; but because of the iniquity that he has committed, he shall die. 14 Again, when I say to the wicked, 'You shall surely die,' if he turns from his sin and does what is lawful and right, 15 if the wicked restores the pledge, gives back what he has stolen, and walks in the statutes of life without committing iniquity, he shall surely live; he shall not die. 16 None of his sins which he has committed shall be remembered against him; he has done what is lawful and right; he shall surely live." (Ezekiel 33:12-16)

In the above two references, the first set of Scripture warns that if the messenger fails to deliver God's warning, the curse will fall upon him for not obeying the Lord. But, it also says the messenger is absolved of any wrong-doing if he delivers the Word and the receiver ignores the warning. In that case, the sword falls upon the one to whom it was given.

The last reference addresses presumption. I have seen this scenario applied to Christians over and over who think their salvation in Christ protects them from the sword. It...does...not!

Consequently, when anyone violates God's spiritual laws, the sword MUST COME. God is honor-bound to His Word concerning this. No amount of religious babbling about binding and loosening, rebuking and decreeing, including all the rigors of anointing by oil, or declaring various Scriptures of deliverance and protection can remove the sword. The ONLY way the sword is removed is by confession, repentance, and restitution.

Removing the Sword

Removing The Sword

The first step to removing the sword is recognizing the violation and the harm done to others. When multiple spiritual laws are violated, it can be complicated. But, in every case, the sword can be removed. This, of course, does not stop the government of sin. As in David's house, sometimes the cause-and-effect is anguishing. But, with the sword removed, one can advance forward.

Once the violation is recognized, the sin must be confessed before the Father. Next, an assessment must be considered as to the extent of damage. Who or how many people were hurt in the violation? The offender must go to them and ask for forgiveness.

> *"Confess your faults one to another, and pray one for another, that you may be healed. The effectual fervent prayer of a righteous man avails much."* (James 5:16)

When it comes to relationships between one another and our Father, the instructions given by Jesus are strongly emphasized:

> *"Therefore if you are presenting your offering at the altar, and there remember that your brother has something against you, leave your offering there before the altar and go, first be reconciled to your brother and then come present your offering."* (Matthew 5:23)

Reconciliation is a serious matter. The Lord desires peace in His house. And even though He loves us, if we hold enmity against a brother or sister in Christ, He rejects our gift. We are rejected when we lift bloody hands in our offerings of prayer, praise, and worship. Briefly stated, God does not honor our presence before Him when we are in willful variance with one another.

It is a very serious violation to strive with members of Christ's Body and partake in the Lord's communion. The Scripture issues a stern warning on this matter:

> *"For anyone who eats and drinks without recognizing the* [requirement concerning the] *body, eats and drinks judgment on himself. 30 That is why many among you are weak and sick, and*

Removing the Sword

a number of you have fallen asleep [died]. *Now if we judged ourselves properly, we would not come under judgment…"* (1 Corinthians 11:29-31. Square brackets added by author for clarity.)

"If possible, so far as it depends on you, be at peace with all men." (Romans 12:17)

Notice that it says, "…so far as it depends on you…". In other words, if the offended person rejects your effort of reconciliation, you are free from further obligation except for issues of restitution.

> **The first step to the removing a sword is to recognize the violation that licensed it along with the scope of its damages.**

When possible, restitution must be made. As in matters of death or when damages exceed one's ability to pay, some things cannot be restored. However, insofar as you are *able*, restitution must be made.

Specific to each person that was violated, forgiveness must be sought within the realm of reasonableness. Seeking forgiveness must be open and transparent, forthright, and honest. Was a church violated? Then forgiveness must be asked in front of the church. It must be in person whenever possible.

Was a family violated? Then your request must be made before the family. Basically, the platform of the violation is the platform of your confession and restitution.

Unacceptable Approaches

Impersonal communication is the new normal. Many business platforms no longer use people to communicate with their customers. Instead, computers do the talking with voice-activated recognition. Problems are resolved through website options or by email exchanges.

Removing the Sword

People text and email in order to avoid face-to-face and eye-to-eye contact. Such communication is succinct, minimum, and without feeling.

In God's Kingdom, however, the transparency of communication does not change.

"Hiding and avoiding" by the means of texting is not a Scripturally acceptable standard, especially when it is possible, although inconvenient, to meet face-to-face:

> *"If your brother or sister sins, <u>go and point out their fault, just between the two of you</u>. If they listen to you, you have won them over."* (Matthew 18:15. Underline by author for added emphasis.)

Scripture instructs us to "go to the person". It is to be a face-to-face interactive conversation in the physical presence of one another, not by remote exchanges over the Internet, or by texting, or phone calls, or exchanges of emails—all of which can be forms of hiding when we want to avoid direct contact.

If it is not practical or possible to meet in person, then, of course, we resort to the next best means of personal interaction. For instance, in the Book of Acts we find repetitive instances where Paul went to the churches and handled the problems. Usually, he sent a personal letter by a chosen courier before he came in person.

Would he have used the Internet if it was available in his day? Absolutely! But, just as he sent letters, he also made personal visits. Yet, despite the rudimentary modes of travel in his day, he never used tactics of "avoidance" or cowardly ways to resolve issues.

The Sword Is Gone, but The Government Continues

As a police officer, I saw many people give their lives to Christ. Sadly, at the same time I watched the government of their sin continue. This is perhaps one of the most painful aspects of the sword. Yes, Satan's license is removed by the blood of Jesus, but the after-effect of sin remains.

Removing the Sword

EXAMPLE: Jane Fonda betrayed the trust of American POWs in Viet Nam whom she visited as a celebrity. They managed to place tiny crumpled notes in her hand without the guards seeing anything. But instead, Jane Fonda handed them to the prison guards. This resulted in the torture and beatings of our POWs.

Years later she gave her life to Jesus. However, her betrayal against our American POWs remains as a permanent tattoo on her life. Yes, Jesus forgave her, but the government of her sin as an American traitor is synonymous with her name.

Other Examples

Speaking confidently from his heart, Peter told Jesus that he would never forsake Him. But Jesus told him that before the rooster crowed, Peter would disown Him three times (Matthew 26:69-75). Even though Jesus lovingly restored him, Peter's painful record is memorialized in Scripture for all generations to read.

> *"Hiding" and "avoiding" by the means of texting does not meet the standard of Scripture when confronting a brother of sister in Christ.*

David's adultery with Bathsheba and the murder of her husband was forgiven, however, the Lord said the sword would never depart from David's house (2 Samuel 12:10). David would see instances of incest, rape, murder, and sedition that plagued his family. The account is forever written in Scripture.

The Holy Spirit told Paul *not* to set foot in Jerusalem. Paul disobeyed Him, ignored the prophetic warning, was subsequently arrested, and kept in prison. He was forgiven, but the government of his sin remained. For over two years he was kept in house-arrest under armed guards. This limited his ability to minister to the Body of Christ at large (Acts 21:4).

Paul's letters to the Ephesians, Philippians, Colossians, and Philemon are known the "prison" epistles because they were written by Paul during his first imprisonment mentioned as in Acts 28.

Removing the Sword

Even though Jesus is our Lord and Savior, our salvation does not remove the penalty of the sword. This must be removed by our confession of sin and any restitution where required. For this reason, walk carefully by the Holy Spirit in order to avoid such consequences.

Where is God's Love in All of This?

God's love for us never wanes or changes. Unfortunately, many people misapply the truth of His love. Naïve and carnal Christians often think that His love shields them from the consequences of His spiritual laws. However, repetitive examples throughout Scripture refute this presumption.

> God's love for us does not invalidate the sword of His Word when we violate His spiritual laws.

Before and *after* David's atrocious sins, God loved him, but the sword remained. And while the sword continued in David's family, David loved the Lord. In fact, after David died, God referred to David's loyal heart as a standard for other Jewish kings to follow. God told them, "If you serve Me as David..." (2 Kings 14:3).

Again, despite God's great love for us, His love does not invalidate the sword of His Word if we violate His spiritual laws. However, because He loves us, we have confidence that if we confess our sins, He will forgive us and restore us. Our restoration requires repentance and restitution, not just confession. From there, He shows us what we must do and how to move forward. But again, the government of our sin remains.

What If I Don't Seek Forgiveness From Others?

Forgiveness is not required from those who have nothing to do with the violation. Nor are you required to address the issue to unrelated parties. However, it is a direct violation of God's Word to ignore or dismiss the requirement of asking for forgiveness of those who were directly affected. Ignoring this leaves the sword in place.

> "So if you are presenting your offering at the altar, and while there you remember that your brother has something

Removing the Sword

[such as a grievance or legitimate complaint] against you, leave your offering there at the altar and go. First make peace with your brother, and then come and present your offering."(Matthew 5:23-24. The Amplified Bible)

His Word says that if your brother has something against you (implying that you are guilty), in so far as it depends on you, you must leave your gift at the altar and reconcile the offense.

Some might call this legalism—that it conveys God as being cold, austere, and without compassion. But remember: His spiritual laws govern without bias. They operate as rulers to ensure blessings as much as a sword.

But All Things Seem to Be Working Out

In the general sense, the sword's penalty does not produce chaos in every sector of one's life. It cuts specific to the violation. Nonetheless, its judgment brings great pain. The correlating cause-and-effect of the penalty is often hidden until it becomes obvious.

As David struck Uriah's family, the sword struck David's family.

The assistant pastor that split his senior pastor's church went through multiple church splits. The sword cut specifically to the offense.

Those who trouble God's house and His children, will suffer trouble in their homes and with their children.

Based on what a person aligns with, the outcome is either a curse or a blessing. There is no neutral area. It is right, or it is wrong.

STORY: After King Saul died in battle, David took the throne of Israel during which a famine had been present for three consecutive years. Because famine is often associated with judgment, David enquired of the Lord as to the reason why there was no rain. The Lord told him it was because of Saul's bloody house and what he did to the Gibeonites. Had David not fasted and sought the Lord's wisdom, the sword's cause-and-effect, manifesting as a mystery-famine, would have continued consuming the land.

Removing the Sword

The Gibeonites were a clan of non-Jewish people. After seeing how God destroy Jericho, they voluntarily surrendered to the Israelites with a covenant agreement. Joshua agreed to their terms and made them slaves to do all the woodcutting and carrying water [6]for the Lord's tabernacle (Joshua 9:4-5). But Saul's "bloody" house violated the covenant. Consequently, the sword was set against Israel in the form of famine.

David went to the Gibeonites and asked what they required to resolve Saul's offense against them (2 Samuel 21:1). They asked for seven sons of Saul's house to be hung before the Lord in Gibeah. Gibeah was Saul's birthplace and his residence when he was king.

David took two sons from Rizpah's house and five sons of Merab's house and gave them to the Gibeonites who promptly hung them. But, the famine continued (2 Samuel 21:8-9).

Did not David enact justice for Saul's sins? Yes! However, he did not complete everything in righteousness that was required of him. What was missing?

According to Jewish law, he was required to *bury* the bodies. He had to bury the sons, not just stack them on the ground. All things had to be completed in righteousness. It was not until *after* David did *all* that was required of him that God received his prayer and removed the famine (2 Samuel 21:9-14).

✱✱✱

Spiritual laws were set into motion by Saul when he was king, but David was responsible to correct them. According to **The Spiritual Law of Dignitary Authority** David, as the new king, was responsible for correcting the wrong done by Saul.

The mandate to govern righteously falls under **The Spiritual Law of Dignitary Authority**. This means that he who stands in a place of responsibility such as a father, husband, pastor, leader of a country, etcetera, assumes righteous responsibility. Even though David did not commit the wrong, by standing in **Dignitary Authority** as king, he was responsible for the sword that Saul set against the land.

---

[6] Joshua 9:1-27

Removing the Sword

People in dignitary positions have direct standing before the throne of God with their prayers.

People in dignitary positions have direct standing before God with their prayers. Thus, parents, as dignitary authority over their children, have persuasion before God when they pray for their children; a president or king, as dignitary authority, have persuasion before God when praying for their country; pastors, as dignitary authority, have persuasion before God when praying for their church. This is because God holds them exclusively accountable to govern in righteousness. To those whom the Lord holds accountable, He grants privilege and preference regarding their prayers.

STORY: When I took the pastorate of a certain church, I sensed something was wrong about the church. The church had a long history of pastors that resigned after an average of two years or less—usually because of schism and division within the congregation members.

I knew there was a hidden sword, but I didn't know on what cause. I sought the elderly people in the church for information and learned that in 1949, well before I was born, the church I was pastoring split from another church.

I went to the church that our church split from over seven decades earlier and asked if they had any information about the issue. No one on their staff was alive at that time. Three times I went to the church and enquired. Finally, one of the secretaries went to a closet and retrieved a small pamphlet entitled, <u>The Hundred Year History of the First Baptist Church</u>. The book detailed the very painful split which was caused by members of the Women's Missionary Society who rallied against the new pastor because they did not agree with how he allocated the missionary funds.

As their grumbling spread, the spirit of transfer worked its way through the congregation. Eventually, sixty-eight key members split from the congregation and started a new church. Little did they know, the foundation of their new church was established on a Jezebel spirit by the women that operated through strife and sedition. According to **The Spiritual Law of Continuity**, the way they left their church is the way they began their new church. Their seditious spirit transferred into their new work. They escaped nothing.

I spoke with the senior pastor of the church that our church split from. I asked if my church, by proxy, could come to his church and asked for forgiveness for what happened in 1949.

On the first Sunday of the coming new year, which was only a few weeks away, I and my congregation attended the other church. I stood in their pulpit and asked forgiveness for what the sixty-eight people did who were aligned with a Jezebel spirit. Following that, we had a mutual water baptism with their church and ours.

I didn't realize, however, that the seditious root in my own church still needed to be destroyed. The offense was forgiven, but the Jezebel spirit needed casting out.

Later, on two separate occasions, two different groups rose up against me, both led by women; both inspired by the same Jezebel spirit that split the other church in 1949.

In the first split, a leading woman who was our worship director spread heretical doctrine through a book written by Matthew Kapler entitled <u>Clash of the Covenants</u>. Kapler's teaching claimed that Jesus and Paul disagreed on the truth of grace. Kapler's audacious claim portrays the most preeminent apostle as an arrogant self-exalted religionist that dared to contest the righteousness of Jesus! In truth, it revealed Kapler as a false teacher who cast aside truth in order to aggrandize his demonic doctrines.

According to the Kapler's heretical teaching, Jesus and Paul had contesting opinions on grace.[7] Kapler's heresy is so incredibly audacious that only a spiritually blind person would fall for his error.

When I showed the woman Kapler's inordinately high number of heretical positions that were scattered throughout his book, she refused to listen. The book she had passed around my church asserted that

---

[7] Kapler, Michael C., Clash of the Covenants, 2018 (self-published) Page 79, "This leaves us with no other choice but to conclude that Paul and Jesus had conflicting opinions and must have agreed to disagree."

Removing the Sword

Christians were under no law of any kind. I showed her God's spiritual laws and how Kapler's teachings were influenced by the doctrines of devils.

She disagreed and confidently asserted that his teachings were true. Then, to use a ridiculous example that was consistent with Kapler's heresy, I asked her if she could engage in unceasing continuous adulterous affairs for the rest of her life and keep her salvation. Without hesitation, she emphatically affirmed that she could because the law had no effect upon her life since she was under grace.

Realizing that she was unteachable, unapproachable, and had no interest in hearing the truth, I asked her not to spread Kapler's doctrine in the church or distribute his book which she had already given to several members of the worship team that she was grooming.

She was immediately angry, slammed her hands on the table and said she was leaving the worship team. She then called those that aligned with her and lied to them by saying I kicked her out of the church. This infuriated them, the very ones who were seduced by Kapler's heretical teaching.

Two years later, another woman in the church rose up. She was part of the first group with the worship director. However, she had conditionally recanted her ways. Unfortunately, the root remained in her and she fell back into rebellion. She subsequently gathered five more women who joined her in the same seditious spirit under the pretense of a personal offense. Again, it was by women carrying the same spirit of Jezebel who, like the two previous groups, refused to handle the matter according to the instructions of God's Word. Consequently, the usurping spirit of Jezebel again sought dominance and attacked the pastor.

As I discovered in prayer, the next step was to rededicate the church to the Lord. This was the first time the church was dedicated to God *after* the sword was removed—seventy-five years later! In so doing, it broke the seditious cycles that found root through a Jezebel spirit!

★★★

Because I stood in Dignitary Authority, I brought the women before the Lord and asked for God's righteous judgment in the matter. This

Removing the Sword

was not to appease my anger, but to show the church that God takes exception with those who trouble His house.

The record now stands as proof of the sword in their lives. They are diminished in spirit, scattered, divided against one another, troubled in their families, lost jobs, spiritually mismatched, stifled in their spiritual depth and progress, and basically just wandering.

God holds the pastor responsible for what he allows in the church, especially when it comes to erroneous doctrine. The Scripture is very clear that the sword cuts both ways: to the pastor for allowing such doctrine, and to those that spread it:

> *"Obey your* [spiritual] *leaders and submit to them, for they keep watch over your souls as those who will give an account. Let them do this with joy and not grief, for this would be unprofitable for you."* (Hebrews 13:17. Square brackets added by author for clarity.)

If, therefore, God holds the pastor accountable as a spiritual leader, then He also holds the people accountable who stand against his authority. This spiritual law brings either blessings or the sword, especially to those that trouble the faith of others.

※
If, God holds the pastor accountable as His spiritual leader, then He also holds the people accountable who stand against the pastor's authority.
※

If the pastor is wrong, the Lord will deal with him directly. God, however, does not permit others to make that judgment or rise up against His church.

As for those that aligned with Jezebel's sedition, the sword remains operational in their lives. Sadly, they have no spiritual understanding or comprehension of such truths. Based on the spiritual laws which they pridefully violated, in their spiritual blindness they are unable to correlate their troubles with the sword. Sadly, they will keep repeating the same pattern that previously existed in their life for many years.

Removing the Sword

Even though most things might appear normal in their daily routines, they have no concept why their anointing is suppressed, stymied, stifled, and basically left on the shelf. Nomadically, they will wander in the spirit and go from one defeat to another without making headway. Until they deal with the sword, their dreams and ambitions remain stalled forever.

Removing the sword requires that they face their sin; humbly seek forgiveness from each person they wounded; and if there is any restitution, make the corrections.

STORY: A pastor and his wife from the eastern states felt called to join my church. They came with strong recommendations and I graciously accepted them into the congregation and on staff with our leadership team. He was a humble man with a very accurate prophetic gifting. His wife, however, was insecure and continuously needed spiritual validation. In truth, she sought control and dominance through her husband by a Jezebel spirit. In stealth, she worked under the pretense of her husband's covering. At the same time, she was aggressively critical of other ministry leaders. She frequently boasted about rebuking this leader or that leader for various things. She proudly touted herself as a bold righteous voice for the Lord.

It happened one day that I and my assistant pastor were counseling a middle-aged single woman in the church. The new assistant pastor's wife came strutting into the office and began accusing me of "beating up the sheep". She arrogantly claimed that the lady we were counseling needed a covering.

True to the character of a Jezebel spirit, she boldly tried to usurp my authority and appoint herself as the woman's covering—a woman she was grooming as one of her followers. She then chided me for not talking to her husband (which was not true).

I replied that the woman who was being counseled had a spiritual covering, and that I and the assistant pastor were present. I told her that her words and actions were highly inappropriate; and that she could speak with me in private. I then asked her to leave the office. She ignored me as she stood behind the woman while caressing her head and hugging her. I abruptly got up and left. She beckoned me back, but I threw up my hands and walked out of the building. As I

Removing the Sword

walked through the door, I felt the Lord's anger and He said in firm Words, "I will deal with her."

Later that afternoon, I received a phone call from her husband who told me that his wife was not feeling well. He asked me and my assistant pastor to come to his house and pray for her. I graciously accepted his request and went to their home.

When we entered the house, his wife was sitting very demurely at the kitchen table. We gathered about her and started praying. Her husband took the lead. While he was praying, I silently said to the Lord that I forgave her for her arrogant display and false accusations. The Lord, however, spoke very firmly to me:

"This isn't about you and her. I have warned her on many occasions not to touch My servants. She would not listen, and I have judged her."

The sword was drawn.

Within two days, half of her face sagged in paralysis and stayed that way for three full years. She humbly admitted that it was a judgment from the Lord for standing against me as the pastor. In truth, it was not just me that the Lord vindicated, but all His servants that she violated with her Jezebel spirit.

Part II

The Spiritual Laws

Chapter Six
The Spiritual Laws

"All Scripture is inspired by God and profitable for teaching, for reproof, for correction, for training in righteousness 17 so that the man of God may be adequate, equipped for every good work." (2 Timothy 3:16-17)

It would take an extended effort to list and explain all the spiritual laws found in Scripture. Accordingly, I am highlighting the ones we deal with most commonly. I am certain, however, that by reading the *primary laws* you can study the Scriptures and easily recognize others for yourself.

As previously stated, the infrastructure of God's Kingdom operates according to His spiritual laws. And even though they are different than the moral and ethical commandments, His spiritual laws superintend and rule over all of His commandments with a sword for disobedience, or blessings by compliance.

As mentioned several times throughout this book, His laws are composed of *natural* and *spiritual* laws. In all cases, they are invisible and work silently. Often their *cause-and-effect* is challenging to identify. Such was the case of the assistant pastor that did not know why his church kept splitting.

Gravity can't be seen, but its effect is easily proven by a bouncing ball. Every bird and airplane that flies through the air is governed by the same invisible laws of aerodynamics.

The Spiritual Laws

Less obvious, but just as real, are God' spiritual laws in the 4th dimension. They literally rule, govern, and regulate the natural world, including our successes and limits in life.

Spiritually mature Christians recognize and understand the importance of God's spiritual laws. They are the governing influences known as "rulers". Such laws work as a light unto our path (Pslam119:105).

Mindful obedience to God's spiritual laws does not make a Christian legalistic. Rather, it makes them wise and understanding as to how God's Kingdom works according to His wisdom.

Immature Christians

The phrase "immature Christian" is simply a term that describes a person's level of maturity in Christ. Typically, immature Christians are carnal, soul-driven, idealistic, and undisciplined.

Sadly, some Christians remain as spiritual infants most of their life. They have little or no concern for God's Kingdom or how it operates. Bluntly stated, they don't care. Accordingly, 1 Corinthians 3:1-3 and in Hebrews 5:12, describe them as follows:

> *"And I, brethren, could not speak to you as to spiritual people* [mature] *but as to carnal, as to babes in Christ. 2 I fed you with milk and not with solid food; for until now you were not able to receive it, and even now you are still not able; 3 for you are still carnal* [immature]. *For where there are envy, strife, and divisions among you, are you not carnal and behaving like mere men?"*
> *(1 Corinthians 3:1-3. Square brackets added by author for clarity.)*

> *"For though by this time you ought to be teachers, you need someone to teach you again the first principles of the oracles of God; and you have come to need milk and not solid food."* *(Hebrews 5:16)*

The insights and revelations of God's spiritual laws appear throughout Scripture in three formats:

The Spiritual Laws

(1) **By the definitive Written Word of God**—those which are plainly set forth in their most literal wording throughout the Bible.

(2) **By examples**—those which are displayed by the actions of people and their resulting consequences.

(3) **By principles**—those which are consistently conveyed through situations and circumstances.

Some of God's spiritual laws have already been addressed. However, for the sake of thoroughness, I will touch on them once more.

The Primary Laws

The first three spiritual laws are the PRIMARY SPIRITUAL LAWS upon which *all* of God's spiritual laws function.

Primary Law #1
The Spiritual Law of the Seed (Genesis 1:11)

All things must produce after their kind. There is no variance or exception to this rule. The type of seed sown defines the type of harvest. It is simple as that—uncomplicated.

Many times we underestimate the seriousness of our actions and fail to realize how a single seed can change the course of our life, sometimes to the good, and sometimes to our grief.

STORY: I was sitting in a church in Denver, Colorado, where I was a guest speaker and the man next to me was poorly dressed. He wore a stained white shirt and faded black slacks; he had no socks, but he was wearing well-used black dress shoes. The Lord spoke to me to give him one of my suits. I thought about which one and the Lord halted my thinking. He instructed me to give him *my best suit*, a gray one, the new one my parents had recently purchased for me. Because it had great sentimental value, I hesitated. When I got back to my hotel room, I decided to do as the Lord told me.

I returned for the evening service and gave the man my suit, a new shirt, belt, t-shirt, and socks. (My shoes would not fit him as we had different size feet.) After giving everything to him, I learned he was

The Spiritual Laws

an African king that the missionaries picked up in a remote village. They brought him to America for a medical operation on his legs.

After finishing my speaking engagement in Denver, I flew to Tulsa, Oklahoma and met with some friends in the ministry. On the way, I had a stop-over in Dallas, Texas. Much to my surprise, my sister met me at the airport and greeted me with *two* brand new suits, shirts, ties, socks, and shoes! I was amazed. She did not know I had just sown my best suit into the African king's life.

When I arrived at Tulsa, I was visiting a friend who took me to the house of a wealthy man in the city. We talked for a bit and he asked me to stand up. Then he came over and stood next to me. Not understanding his strange ploy, we all laughed.

He left the room and a few minutes later returned with thirteen brand new tailor-made suits he had fashioned for himself. He explained that he suddenly felt led to bless me with them. He had no idea why. He said it just seemed like the right thing to do. I laughed and told him the story.

There is an inverse to this as well. What if I had not listened to the Lord? What if I had dismissed the Holy Spirit's leading? I would have lost the blessing which God desired to give me. I would have one suit instead of fifteen. Conversely, how many times do we miss blessings which cannot be calculated because we dismiss the Lord's leading?

★★★

The seed-type you sow is the harvest-type you reap. Primary Law #1 is **The Spiritual Law of the Seed**. Each seed produces after its own kind. Therefore, give careful consideration as to the seeds you plant, either by acts of *commission*, or in some cases, acts of *omission*.

Your words and actions are seeds. They MUST return to you. It is an immutable law.

An act of *omission* is when something should have been said or done but was not acted upon.

Do you want mercy in your life? Then give mercy.
Do you want sadness in your life? Then cause sadness.

The Spiritual Laws

Do you want peace in your life? Then cause peace.
Do you want favor in your life? Then give favor.
Do you want blessings in life? Then bless others.

> "So then, in everything treat others the same way you want them to treat you, for this is [the essence of] the Law and the [writings of the] Prophets." (Matthew 7:12. Square brackets added by author for clarity.)

What do you want in life? How do you want people to treat you? What you do to others invariably and absolutely returns to you.

Primary Law #1
The seed-type you sow becomes the harvest-type you reap. This is The Spiritual Law of the Seed.

If you ignore people's needs when it is within your ability to help, you will be ignored when you are in need (acts of omission.) On the other hand, if you give mercy, respect, grace, and kindness, it will return to you as a harvest.

> "Treat others the same way you want them to treat you."
> (Luke 6:31)

According to the Primary Law #1, the harvest we reap is the seeds we have sown.

> "So the LORD has repaid me according to my righteousness, according to the cleanness of my hands in His sight 25 To the faithful, You show Yourself faithful, to the blameless, You show yourself blameless. 26 to the pure, You show Yourself pure, but to the crooked, You show Yourself shrewd." (Psalm 18:24-26)

Primary Law #2
The Spiritual Law of Sowing and Reaping

This links directly to the first law, **The Spiritual Law of the Seed**. As already explained, **The Law of Sowing and Reaping** warns that God is not mocked (Galatians 6:7). A person *must* reap whatever they

The Spiritual Laws

sow. It is immutable; it cannot be broken; it is invariable. A return MUST come.

You must reap what you sow. But remember: according to **The Spiritual Law of Manifold Return**, whatever you sow returns in *greater* quantity. This is why Jesus said it is more blessed to give than receive (Acts 20:35). For this reason, obedience assures increase, blessings, and promotions!

However, there is a sober warning pertaining to this spiritual law: The default of NOT sowing when you should, is the harvest of having *nothing* in your day of need.

<u>**Primary Law #2**</u>
The Law of Sowing and Reaping warns that God is not mocked. Whatever a person sows, they will reap. It is immutable. It cannot be broken. It is invariable and a return MUST come.

At the same time, sowing the **wrong seed** brings a manifold harvest of grief. Conversely, sowing the **right seed** brings a manifold harvest of joy and blessing.

The promise of increase is simply this: consistently sowing righteousness produces a consistent abundance of blessings with increased favor.

Faith Is Not Required

As previously stated, faith is not required for God's spiritual laws to work. They are sovereign governing authorities that rule and superintend all things regardless of anyone's belief. Therefore, it is imperative that we understand and know God's laws. By His wisdom, we can properly apply them and reap His blessing.

If we act with indifference or with reckless actions by doing as we please, the sword is guaranteed. Therefore, in whatever you do, act on the side of mercy. On this cause, the Apostle James is very clear when the Lord says:

The Spiritual Laws

"And the seed whose fruit is righteousness is sown in peace by those who make peace." (James 3:18)

Primary Law #3
The Spiritual Law of Manifold Returns

This was touched upon in the Primary Law #2. But know for certain that everything sown returns in manifold increase. Our faithful gracious Heavenly Father sowed Jesus and reaped many sons in return. Whatever is sown as a single seed returns in manifold quantity. This is why the tithe and offering always yields more than what is sown. For this reason, the Bible records Paul's words:

> *"In everything I [Paul] showed you that by working hard in this manner you must help the weak and remember the words of the Lord Jesus, that He Himself said, 'It is more blessed to give than to receive.'"* (Acts 20:35. Square brackets added by author for clarity.)

This spiritual law assures increase according to what we sow. It includes actions of faithfulness, loyalty, endurance, and steadfastness. These are the foundational-virtues of every champion according to **The Laws of Spiritual Advancement**.

Whatever is sown comes back in a greater ratio of blessing. And whatever is withheld by acts of omission, returns in greater loss.

In the same way, this law wields a sword. Those who sow discord, strife, and dishonesty must reap the same according to the seeds they plant.

The vices of unfaithfulness, disloyalty, and patterns of resignation are deficiencies in the constitution of a person's character. They permeate throughout one's life which makes a person untrustworthy, non-advancing, troubled, and often confused. For this reason, people that lack endurance and steadfastness are trained quitters when things get difficult. They see no value in sacrifice and faithfulness. Nor do they understand the laws of promotion. For this reason, they seldom rise to victory but instead live with limitation and defeat.

> *"Now He who supplies seed for sowing and bread for food will supply your seed for sowing and increase the harvest of your*

The Spiritual Laws

righteousness; 11 you will be enriched in everything for all liberality, which through is producing thanksgiving to God." (2 Corinthians 9:10-11)

In the above Scripture, Paul encouraged the Corinthian Christians to prepare a gift for the poorer churches. But notice that it never mentions money. This is because Paul was speaking of **The Spiritual Law of Manifold Returns** which applies to *any* type of seed sown.

"Give [in anything thing tangible or intangible] *and it will be given* [back] *to you. They* [the laws that govern] *will pour into your lap a good measure pressed down, shaken together, and running over. For by the standard of measure it will be measured back to you." (Luke 6:38. Square brackets added by author for clarity.)*

Primary Law #3
Every seed returns in manifold increase. A single seed always produces more than itself.

These three primary spiritual laws work in a compounding simultaneous action with other spiritual laws. For example, the spiritual laws of communication, agreement, alignment, confession, and transfer all work in concert. At the same time, they stand alone as governing laws.

The Spiritual Laws of Communication, Agreement, Alignment, Confession, and Transfer

Chapter Seven
The Spiritual Laws of Communication, Agreement, Alignment, Confession, and Transfer

"A good man's speech reveals the treasures within him. An evil-hearted man is filled with venom, and his speech reveals it. 36 And I tell you this, that you must give an account on Judgment Day for every idle word you speak. 37 Your words now reflect your fate then: either you will be justified by them or you will be condemned." (Matthew 12:35-37)

The Concert of Five Spiritual Laws

As previously stated, God's spiritual laws are an interrelated network that connect one law to another. For example, the Three Primary Laws of the seed always work in concert: (1) every seed produces; (2) every seed produces after its own kind; (3) every seed produces more than itself.

In the same principle of interrelationship, the spiritual laws of communication, agreement, alignment, confession, and transfer work in concert. These five spiritual laws always work in sequence of one connecting to the other. At the same time, each part stands as an individual spiritual law. For instance, there is no agreement without

The Spiritual Laws of Communication, Agreement, Alignment, Confession, and Transfer

communication, and without agreement, there is no power. Communication comes *before* agreement. Power comes *after* agreement.

> "Again I say to you, that if two believers on earth agree [that is, are of one mind, in harmony] about anything that they ask [within the will of God], it will be done for them by My Father in heaven." (Matthew 18:19. Square brackets added by author for clarity.)

Salvation is the process of five spiritual laws. First, the Gospel is **communicated** and then received in **agreement** based on the truth. After agreement, the person **aligns** with God's truth. His truth is **confessed**, and the person is **transferred** into a new life.

By whatever means communication is conveyed, whether by speech, writing, dreams, or visions, it must be understood in order for there to be agreement.

Satan understands the process of these spiritual laws, especially how power comes through agreement by **The Spiritual Law of Communication**.

According to John 8:44, there is no truth in Satan. Truth is Satan's worst enemy. In contrast, Jesus said that truth makes people free (John 8:32). Therefore, Satan monitors all forms of **communication** in order to steal the truth before it becomes power by **agreement**. We see this strategy in the parable of the seed when the seed of God's Word is stolen to prevent **agreement** before it produces power.

> "When anyone hears the message about the kingdom and does not understand it, the evil one comes and snatches away what was sown in their heart. This is the seed sown along the path." (Matthew 13:9)

Every form of **communication** that comes to us must be judged by the standard of God's written Word. Whatever we see, hear, feel, taste, touch, read, learn, or encounter must be evaluated by God's Spirit within us according to His Word. By the standard of God's

The Spiritual Laws of Communication, Agreement, Alignment, Confession, and Transfer

Word, we can know if it comes from Satan, the spirit of man, or from God.

Destructive seeds gain access into our lives if they are not properly judged according to God's Spirit by His Written Word. For this reason, we are told in Scripture how to conduct our lives:

> *"But He answered and said, 'It is written, 'Man shall not live by bread alone, but by every Word [Rhema] that proceeds from the mouth of God.'"* (Matthew 4:4. Square brackets added by author for clarity.)

God's truths must be received, studied, and meditated upon. They must be weaved into the constitution of our lives by **agreement**. It must be deeper than mere academia—it must be *revelation*. [8]

According to the Jewish perspective of truth, a person does not actually *know* truth until he or she lives it as a principle. Mere mental ascent is only the first step.

STORY: A troubled woman in my church once handed me a letter in a sealed packet. It was filled with angry and scathing accusations. As she tossed the packet on the table in front of me, instantly the Lord said in a clear warning: "Do not open it! She thinks her words are from Me. This did not come from My Spirit. They were crafted in darkness as words of Satan to vex your soul."

I immediately picked up the packet, handed it to one of our leaders, and told him to throw it away. I did this as proof that I never opened myself to her dark words which were influenced by a Jezebel spirit operating in concert with another woman.

This particular woman frequently fronted a spiritually sensitive image and regularly testified about her subjective experiences in the mystical realm. She claimed she smelled fragrances during

---

[8] The Jewish picture of meditation is a cow that grazes all day then lies upon the grass to chew the cud.

The Spiritual Laws of Communication, Agreement, Alignment, Confession, and Transfer

heightened spiritual moments, saw spirits, colors, and received spiritual signals. Meanwhile, she never walked in peace, but consistently lived a guarded life in suspicion and fear.

Other *Christian* women spirituality **aligned** with her and subtly competed with her claims. She had no idea that Satan used her as an agent of strife and dissension. She properly fit the description of those whom Paul warned about in the Colossian church concerning spiritual experiences that were largely influenced by things other than the Holy Spirit.

> *"Let no one keep defrauding you of your prize by delighting in self-abasement...taking his stand on visions he has seen, inflated without cause by his fleshly mind." (Colossians 2: 18b)*

★★★

We must be quick to scrutinize every **communication** that comes to us. We must be sensitive to the Holy Spirit's leading at all times. Passivity, insensitivity, and walking without a circumspect awareness is like dancing in a mine field.

EXAMPLE: Jesus asked His disciples who people thought He was. Peter answered by a revelation which he received from the Father:

> *"And they said, "Some say John the Baptist; and others, Elijah; but still others, Jeremiah, or one of the prophets." 15 He said to them, "But who do you say that I am?" 16 Simon Peter answered, "You are the Christ, the Son of the living God." 17 And Jesus said to him, "Blessed are you, Simon Barjona, because flesh and blood did not reveal this to you, but My Father who is in Heaven. 18 And I also say to you that you are Peter, and upon this rock I will build My church; and the gates of Hades will not overpower it...22 From that time Jesus began to point out to His disciples that it was necessary for Him to go to Jerusalem and to suffer many things from the elders, chief priests, and scribes, and to be killed, and to be raised up on the third day. Peter took Him aside and began to rebuke Him, saying, "God forbid it, Lord! This shall never happen to You." 23 But He turned and said to Peter, "Get behind Me, Satan! You are a*

The Spiritual Laws of Communication, Agreement, Alignment, Confession, and Transfer

stumbling block to Me; for you are not setting your mind on God's interests, but man's." *(Matthew 16: 14-18,22-23)*

Here, we discover an important insight: An unguarded person can unwittingly switch from one influence to another without recognizing the source. In Peter's case, he went from a direct influence of the Father to a Satanic influence. We must, therefore, be sensitive to the Holy Spirit at all times in order to know which voice or influence is speaking to us.

Jesus quickly recognized the spiritual shift in Peter's words. And even though Peter was Jesus' trusted friend, Jesus trapped Peter's words and immediately annulled them.

Sometimes Words from the Lord are sent as a rebuke or a warning to divert us from disaster. They can sound harsh, direct, and contrary to grace.

Again, we must be alert and sensitive to the quickening of the Holy Spirit when any form of **communication** comes to us, even when it comes from our friends and those we deem trustworthy. Otherwise, things which seem righteous or of no alarm are allowed entry to the soul as seeds of destruction, especially from trusted sources where our guard is down.

The criteria for judging words and actions is not whether you like them or dislike them. Satan often disguises his words with sugar in order to hide the poison. Therefore, **communication** must be judged on the merits of truth. Anything inharmonious with God's Word is NOT truth.

Sometimes God sends words as a rebuke or a warning to turn us from disaster. They can sound harsh, direct, and confronting. In mercy, they warn us to turn from a path of destruction.

EXAMPLE: I once confronted a Christian man who had a lust problem. He was young and handsome, had a lot of charisma, and

The Spiritual Laws of Communication, Agreement, Alignment, Confession, and Transfer

possessed a witty fun personality. But, he was a serial fornicator that moved from woman to woman.

I saw him flirting with a beautiful girl in the church and I sternly warned him by the Holy Spirit. I reminded him of what Jesus said about causing people to stumble: "It would be better for you if a millstone were hung around your neck and you were thrown into the sea than to cause her to stumble with your nefarious disarming tactics of seduction. Touch her, and your life will fall into disarray (Luke 17:2) ". He immediately sobered. God had revealed his intentions, and he affirmed it was a warning from the Lord.

At times, what may sound like a curse spoken in the name of Jesus is actually a warning to save us from Satan's plan. Carnal Christians often react to such warnings and never recognize them as the Lord's mercy.

STORY: While on patrol in the late evening hours, I came upon a vehicle parked behind a building. I quietly drove up to it with my lights off, stepped from my police car, and aimed my 30,000 candlepower flashlight to the inside of the vehicle. Two young people were nearly stripped naked and ready to have sex. Obviously, they were taken by surprise when I shined the flashlight on them. I immediately ordered them out of the vehicle. The girl was fourteen, almost fifteen years old. The boy was seventeen, almost eighteen years old.

I could have arrested them for public indecency, but instead I ordered them to get dressed. I subsequently took her home, presented her to her parents, and explained the context of my encounter. The parents were thankful, but angry. They thought she was spending the night with a girlfriend.

The next day on patrol I saw the young man in a parking lot where his peers typically hung out. In front of a crowd, he brazenly challenged me, knowing, of course, that I would not react to his juvenile bravado. Dismissing his vanity, I gave him stern words of advice:

The Spiritual Laws of Communication, Agreement, Alignment, Confession, and Transfer

"You were eight days away from qualifying for felony statutory rape with a minor under the age of eighteen years old. You are a senior in high school. She is only in ninth grade. If you don't get a handle on your stupidity, you'll get her pregnant. Next year when you start college, you'll have to drop out of school to support her and the baby. You won't get married to her because she is too young. But you'll ruin her education and life by encumbering her with motherhood at a time when she still needs to finish high school and physically grow up. You, however, will be saddled with eighteen years of child support. Unable to afford your college education, you'll end up working at Nemo's bar just to survive. You'll bring undue burden to your life, her life, and your child's life that will never know a normal family model."

He responded with various expletives and I simply walked away. Within six months, exactly everything I said happened. She became a mother in tenth grade. He dropped out of college in his freshman year and took a job working at Nemo's bar to pay for the delivery costs plus the ongoing child support—for eighteen years. They never got married.

Was it a spoken curse, or a warning in the Lord? He controlled the outcome. Standing in arrogance and defiance, he walked directly into the sword and brought grief to the mother and his child.

★★★

When Eve encountered Satan in the garden, he **communicated** lies to her. Without judging his words, she dropped her guard, **agreed** with them, entered into **alignment**, **confessed** his temptation, acted on them, and was **transferred** from life to death. Was it a curse God spoke over Adam and Eve when He previously warned them, or was it a warning to divert them from spiritual death?

> "But from the tree of the knowledge of good and evil you shall not eat, for in the day that you eat from it you will surely die." (Genesis 2:17)

Marriages rise or fall on the factors of **communication**. When **communication** fails, nothing constructive is **agreed** upon and nothing

The Spiritual Laws of Communication, Agreement, Alignment, Confession, and Transfer

is solved. The failure of **communication** eliminates constructive **agreement**. The outcome ends as an **agreement** to "irreconcilable differences".

The Spiritual Law of Communication is a neutral law just like all of God's spiritual laws. The outcome is based on whether the **communication** is true or false. From there, it is either **agreement** or rejection; **alignment** or avoidance; **confession** or denial, and finally, **transference** or refusal.

Cults, for example, are based on lies and deception. Scripture calls them the "doctrines of devils" (1 Timothy 4:1) which Satan manipulates to his own objectives of stealing, killing, and destroying.

People accept the **communication** of demonic doctrines, **agree** with their teachings, **align** with its tenets, **confess** them from the heart, and solidify the **transfer** within their spirit.

In the same principle, church splits are based upon words (**communication**) by **agreement** which produces **alignment** and a common **confession**. From there, the malcontents bond in destructive power as they **transfer** the darkness into their souls. The pattern is the same: **communication agreement, alignment, confession, and transfer**.

To be blessed in this present life, we must listen to the Holy Spirit's voice. Jesus described the Spirit's work in our lives when He said:

> *"But the Helper [Comforter, Advocate, Intercessor, Counselor, Strengthener, Standby], the Holy Spirit, whom the Father will send in My name* [in My place, to represent Me and act on My behalf], *He will teach* [communicate to] *you all things. And He will help you remember* [by His communication] *everything that I have told you."* (John 14:26. The Amplified Bible. Square brackets added by author for clarity.)

God's Word, the Bible, is a guide in every circumstance. His Word and His spiritual laws never contradict each other.

The Spiritual Laws of Communication, Agreement, Alignment, Confession, and Transfer

The Holy Spirit always speaks God's Word. He reveals the perfect will of the Father in all instances. Unfortunately, immature and carnally based Christians have great difficulty distinguishing the Holy Spirit's voice from man's spirit or a spirit of darkness.

Who are these Christians that lack discernment and are used by the agents of darkness? They are easily recognized. They float from church to church. They are unteachable and independent. They are submitted to no one. They disdain Kingdom authority while self-glorifying their own spirituality. They rely heavily upon subjective experiences and constantly look for validation and endorsement.

Such people remind me of a particular woman in my church that repetitively spoke prophetic words about people feeling condemned or carrying false guilts. No one typically responded to her because there was no anointing in what she said. Finally, I approached her and told her that she was speaking from the pains of her own soul, and not from the Spirit of the Lord.

The Power Behind Words

Three million Israelites and their livestock traveled through the open desert as a single congregation. During the day, God went before them as a cloud to shield them from the scorching sun. At night, He was a pillar of fire to give them perfect evening temperatures. Every day He fed them with manna and supplied them with clean, cool, fresh water. Their clothes did not wear out, nor did their feet swell.

> *"Indeed for forty years You sustained them in the wilderness. They lacked nothing. Their clothes did not wear out nor did their feet swell."* (Nehemiah 9:21)

As God's chosen people, their reputation advanced before them. Everywhere the Israelites went, God's power was displayed as an unstoppable force. The fame of His power spread throughout the world, especially concerning Egypt's destruction and how God drowned their entire army in the sea.

The Spiritual Laws of Communication, Agreement, Alignment, Confession, and Transfer

When they came to the region of Moab, King Balak was concerned that the Israelites would destroy them just as they destroyed the Amorites (Numbers 21:21-25). As a countermeasure, he paid the prophet Balaam[9] to speak a curse over them.

> **If words and declarations are nothing more than empty utterances, then of course Israel had nothing to be concerned about and the Lord's intervention was not needed.**

To Balak, a curse carried real power. He understood God's spiritual laws better than most Christians, especially "Westernized Christians".

Satan waited for Balaam's curse as a license to move against the Israelites. Therefore, God warned Balaam to speak only which God told him to say.

This rather lengthy account spans from Numbers chapter 22 through 24. It is a classic model showing how words carry power.

If words and declarations are nothing more than empty utterances, then the Lord's intervention was not needed. But if words carry power, as they do, then words can be weapons.

The age-old rhyme of, "Sticks and stones may hurt my bones, but words will never harm me", is not true!

---

[9] Some Bible expositors claim Balaam was a heathen-diviner with a well-known reputation for accuracy. Balaam, however, claimed his powers came from God Almighty, and it seems he had clear communication with God according to the Scriptures. I take the position that he was in fact a prophet, but like so many ministers today, he was easily persuaded by money. The repeated conversation he had with God indicate his relationship as a prophet. However, due to his prostitution of the gift, he was later denounced as a diviner.

The Spiritual Laws of Communication, Agreement, Alignment, Confession, and Transfer

Realizing the power of words, God withstood Balaam. He did not want His people demonically harassed by curses.

When God Speaks

God reveals His intentions to His prophets in order to guide, direct, prepare, and warn His people:

> *"Surely the Lord God does nothing unless He reveals His secret counsel to His servants, the prophets."* (Amos 3:7)

God declares His plans through His prophets so that His Word is an established record on the earth. His Word, whether it comes from the Bible, or is delivered by an angel, or by anyone speaking through the Spirit of God, cannot be altered.

God often sends His Word through the gifts of the Holy Spirit: Prophecy, The Word of Knowledge, or the Word of Wisdom in order to turn people from destruction. Such words are given as an established record so that when it comes to pass it cannot be construed as mere coincidence, chance, or probability.

> *"Indeed, God speaks once, or twice, yet no one notices it. 15 In a dream, a vision of the night, when sound sleep falls on men, while they slumber in their beds, 16 then He opens the ears of men and seals their instruction, 17 that He may turn man aside from his conduct, and keep man from pride; 18 He keeps back his soul from the pit, and his life from passing over into Sheol"* (Job 33:14-19)

EXAMPLE: At a time in history, Iraq was rich and fertile, a land lush with green vegetation and flowing with water. The nation was described as the "Glory of the Chaldean Pride" and known as a hub of great commerce. The city of Babylon was located in Iraq and hosted the Hanging Gardens—one of the eight wonders of the world. But God sent a prophetic Word against the land:

> *"And Babylon, the beauty of kingdoms, the glory of the Chaldeans' Pride, will be as when God overthrew Sodom and Go-*

The Spiritual Laws of Communication, Agreement, Alignment, Confession, and Transfer

> morrah. 20 *It will never be inhabited or lived in from generation to generation, <u>nor will the Arab pitch his tent there</u>, nor will shepherds make their flocks lie down there. Hyenas will howl in their fortified towers and jackals in their luxurious palaces. Her fateful time will soon come and her days will not be prolonged."*
> (Isaiah 13:19-22. Underline by author for added emphasis.)

Starting from that day in 539 BC, every detail of what God said remains actively in force. Today, the nomadic Arabs will not pitch their tents there overnight. It remains a dry desert and a disheveled ruin never more to be inhabited.

God spoke it. His Word was established as a record. He fulfilled His Word. The prophecy stands as a testimony to His glory.

★★★

According to **The Spiritual Law of Communication**, once God releases His Word, He stands behind it to accomplish precisely every detail of everything He said. He does not speak in approximations to impress. Every Word is specific.

> *"So will the Word be that goes forth out of My mouth; it will not return to Me empty, without accomplishing what I desire, and without succeeding in the matter for which I sent it."* (Isaiah 55:11)

When the Spirit warns someone to turn from a sin, be assured that God will do two things: (1) He will prove His Word according to what He said, and (2) He will vindicate His servant that delivered the Word.

Even if people attack His messengers and refuse His Word, God still requires His servant to deliver it. This is to establish the record that correlates with judgment. From there, **The Spiritual Law of Manifold Returns** comes into play.

> *"See that you do not refuse Him who speaks. For if they did not escape who refused Him who spoke on earth, much more shall we not escape if we turn away from Him who speaks from*

The Spiritual Laws of Communication, Agreement, Alignment, Confession, and Transfer

heaven, 26 whose voice then shook the earth; but now He has promised, saying, "Yet once more I shake not only the earth, but also heaven." 27 Now this, "Yet once more," indicates the removal of those things that are being shaken, as of things that are made, that the things which cannot be shaken may remain. 28 Therefore, since we are receiving a kingdom which cannot be shaken, let us have grace, by which we may serve God acceptably with reverence and godly fear 29. For our God is a consuming fire." (Hebrews 12:25-29)

His messengers carry **Dignitary Authority** when they speak on behalf of God. He warns everyone not to touch His anointed ones and do His prophets no harm. The sword attached to **The Spiritual Law of Dignitary Authority** bears a great penalty. Furthermore, God will surely vindicate His servants!

"He who receives you, receives Me, and he who receives Me, receives Him who sent me. He who receives a prophet in the name of a prophet shall receive a prophet's reward; and he who receives a righteous man in the name of a righteous man shall receive a righteous man's reward." (Matthew 10:39-41)

When a warning in the Spirit is given to divert someone from a consequence, be assured that God will do two things: (1) He will prove His Word according to what He said, and (2) He will vindicate His servant that delivered the Word.

We see another important spiritual law: **The Spiritual Law of Implied Reverse.** This means that when God speaks a Word through His servant, God claims the Word as if He spoke it to them in person. And if God's message, given as a warning, is rejected, then His mercy ends and His judgment begins.

STORY: During my seventy-fourth trip to Ghana, Africa in March of 2020, I was taken to the residence of the former president of Ghana and spoke to him about his campaign for the nation's top office.

The Spiritual Laws of Communication, Agreement, Alignment, Confession, and Transfer

Between March and November of 2020 I had a prophetic Word for the national election chairperson—the person who manages the voting and officially declares the winners. On two separate occasions, I was given a prophetic word and told the chairperson to decide for neither candidate, but in righteousness speak the truth. The assurance was that God would vindicate the chairperson before the people. I was perplexed by the word because I assumed the person could decide nothing but simply read the voting count.

Five months later during my seventy-fifth trip to Ghana on November 2, 2020, I spoke very briefly in a church. I did not realize I was being nationally televised from border to border. I told the congregation that troubling times were coming to Ghana; that according to God's wisdom, the Lord had especially anointed one man to handle the problems. I then mentioned the candidate's name—John Mahama. The church exploded in a chorus of murmurings. It sounded like I struck the side of a wooden apiary—a box for keeping bees.

Many were offended by the prophetic Word. Some denounced it by calling it an opinion, not a prophecy from the Lord. In truth, I knew very little about either candidate, the one sitting in office, or the former president.

Riots broke out across the nation. Unrest filled the country and the Ghana national police shot and killed numbers of unarmed citizens. Following that, furious televised debates erupted with evidence that proved the vote-count was fraudulent. College professors presented the mathematical impossibility of the vote count.

The case was appealed to Ghana's supreme court. Then came ubiquitous allegations that the judges were bribed during the appeal process. Ghana mourned under an oppressive cloud. The sitting president had no anointing from God to handle the problems. Inflation and corruption went out of control. As the economy dropped in strength, businesses shut down all over the nation. Fuel prices doubled. Mistrust in government was everywhere, and the people suffered greatly.

The Spiritual Laws of Communication, Agreement, Alignment, Confession, and Transfer

I returned again to Ghana in March 2022 and discovered that everything spoken by the prophetic utterance had come to pass. Those who objected to the word saw the evidence of God's warning.

★★★

The Spiritual Law of Agreement

Agreement is the power of life. Whenever we **agree** with something, we **align** with it. Understanding this one spiritual law is incredibly important.

The truth makes us free. However, when negatives such as lies, deception, half-truths, and humanist social philosophy is received, there is **alignment** by **agreement** and the sword is unsheathed.

According to The Oxford English Dictionary, the Woke Generation is defined as: "well-informed, up-to-date. Chiefly alert to racial or social discrimination and injustice".

The Woke Generation's humanist philosophy is completely absent of God's righteousness. Under the pretense of "individual rights", they endorse a plethora of issues contrary to God's Word. Thus, the philosophy of their gender identity titles includes male, female, transgender, gender neutral, non-binary, agender, pangender, genderqueer, two-spirit, third gender, all combined, selectively combined, or none at all.

Humanism is the exaltation of man over God. Being absent of God's truth, there is no absolute truth in any individual, society, or culture. This gives Satan exactly what he needs to distort, confuse, and destroy the only part of creation made in God's image—mankind.

According to one study, "Between 2009 and 2017, rates of depression among kids ages fourteen to seventeen increased by more than 60%. The increase was nearly as steep among those ages twelve to thirteen (47%), and eighteen to twenty-one (46%), and the rates roughly doubled among those ages twenty to twenty-one. In 2017—the latest year for which federal data are available—more than one in eight Americans ages

The Spiritual Laws of Communication, Agreement, Alignment, Confession, and Transfer

twelve to twenty-five experienced a major depressive episode, the study found."[10]

These statistics prove the presence of the sword's penalty in this generation—a generation with no absolute moral conscience, direction, or identity.

> Humanism is the credo of the Woke Generation which they hold as a higher value than God's truths. Satan is raising a generation of people without identity and without God's righteousness.

As Satan continues expanding his movement, we must stay vitally connected to God's guiding truths. We must be vigilant and on guard against every encroaching philosophy and dark value communicated through fallacious logic and dark-spirited individualism.

Just as Jesus instantly trapped Peter's words, we must apply God's spiritual laws at the inception of every **communication**. "Principle-based" Christians understand this fundamental truth.

Agreement and **alignment** with God's righteousness produces power. By keeping close fellowship with the Holy Spirit, we are safe under the authority of His Word. Moreover, we are protected as we *confess* our *agreement* with His Word. *Living* His principles is an active **confession** of His truth.

When Paul handed a *backslidden Christian* over to Satan, no one had the power to annul Paul's authority which was given by God's leading. Why? Because it was God's directive—a sword against the man. Consequently, when Satan struck the man's body, no degree of prayer, utterance, binding, loosening, or rebukes could work. God's truth cannot be rebuked. And yet, many immature Christians, absent of God's leading, try to do just that. Based on their

---

[10] https://time.com/5550803/depression-suicide-rates-youth/

The Spiritual Laws of Communication, Agreement, Alignment, Confession, and Transfer

presumption, they have a mis-informed view of God, His ways, principles, and wisdom.

The Spiritual Law of the Implied Reverse is just as powerful. For instance, Jesus said we would know the truth and the truth would make us free (John 8:32). The implied reverse is just as true. If you do not know the truth, bondage and limitation actively remain.

> *"For rebellion is as the sin of divination, and insubordination is as iniquity and idolatry."* (1 Samuel 15:23)

Rebellion against God's Word is like the sin of divination. Divination, in this regard, is to manipulate or persuade by power. It means to influence and engineer an outcome apart from righteousness according to one's lust and desire.

Those who **align** themselves with darkness stand against righteousness. Satan uses them as agents of darkness—including ignorant, immature, and well-meaning Christians. This is commonly known in Scripture as the sin of presumption.

> *"Also keep back Your servant from presumptuous sins; Let them not rule over me; then I will be blameless, and I shall be acquitted of great transgression."* (Psalm 19:13)

> *"With gentleness,* [we are] *correcting those who are in opposition, if perhaps God may grant them repentance leading to the knowledge of the truth, 26 and they may come to their senses and escape from the snare of the devil, <u>having been led captive by him to do his will</u>."* (2 Timothy 2:25-26. Square brackets added by author for clarity.)

The Bible is replete with the names of men and woman who presumptuously opposed God's righteous authority:

- Diotrephes: (3 John 1:9). He wanted the preeminence and focus on himself by asserting that *his* leadership was best.

The Spiritual Laws of Communication, Agreement, Alignment, Confession, and Transfer

- Hymenaeus and Alexander: (1 Timothy 1:9). Both men were Christian teachers in the Ephesian church. However, they were turned over to Satan for preaching heresy because they refused to repent.

- Philetus: (2 Timothy 2:17). He joined in agreement and alignment with Hymenaeus in opposition to Paul. Hymenaeus was evidently a persuasive teacher.

- Demas: (2 Timothy 4:10). He deserted Paul and went back to the world. This was after Demas heard Paul's teachings and saw the miracles that God worked through Paul.

- Jezebel: (Revelation 2:20). She called herself a prophetess but was judged unto death. Evidently, she had supernatural giftings, persuasive speech, and a following in church. Nothing of her works was born of God's Spirit.

Idolatry is a value system. Principally, whatever we value above God and His righteousness is idolatry. In this regard, choosing sin over God is idolatry (1 Corinthians 10:13-15).

The Law of Agreement works either as a blessing or a sword. When used unrighteously, **agreement** can be divination. Satan uses this very principle of **agreement** in the operation of divination in order to enlist forces of evil. Even more surprising, Christians can be used as instruments of such evil, especially when two or three gather together and **agree** to anything *not* of God's will.

But why would any Christian partake in this sin? In a broad sense, such Christians do not know they are being used in this type of violation. This is especially true of idealistic Christians who lack the depth and understanding of God's Word. They are prone to such traps of Satan. By presumption, what sounds right, looks right, or seems right is assumed to be right. To them, what *appears* truthful or righteous can also be diametrically opposed to God's will and Word. This is why the Holy Spirit's leading is vital in all that we do through **agreement**.

The Spiritual Laws of Communication, Agreement, Alignment, Confession, and Transfer

Scripture warns that there is a way which can seem right to a person, but its end is death (Proverbs 16:25). For instance, various cults commonly use the name of Jesus but at the same time deny His divinity. They sound right, appear kind and benevolent, have philanthropic works, build large church buildings, and attract thousands to their doctrines, but, they are in fact, vacuums into hell.

STORY: A young man dated a pageant queen for a few years and they discussed the possibility of getting married. Even though he walked honorably before the Lord, her church took exception to their relationship. He was a Spirit-filled Christian, however, her church aggressively opposed the Baptism of the Holy Spirit. According to their belief, he was deceived and spiritually skewed. As such, they feared she would be led astray by his doctrine.

Certain women in her church routinely gathered to pray against the relationship which is aptly described, in this application, as Christian divination. These same "prayer warriors" had no comprehension of the young man's positive moral influence with his girlfriend. They failed to comprehend how his anointing was a type of covering over her in their relationship. Nonetheless, the couple ultimately broke up because of intervening spiritual conflicts.

Within a few months after the breakup, she cast off all moral restraint and delved into licentious sexual sin. Eventually, she ended up pregnant and aborting the child. Later, she had four more children from different men, including one child by a married man that broke up his marriage. She ultimately ended up in prison for running drugs and endured a greatly troubled life before coming back to the Lord.

It is interesting that her church censured the Spirit-filled Christian man's faith. But they did nothing when the young woman fell into destructive abhorrent lifestyles of sin. In their efforts to break up the relationship, they **aligned** themselves by **agreement** and destroyed the relationship with spiritual divination.

★★★

The Spiritual Laws of Communication, Agreement, Alignment, Confession, and Transfer

Christians Used in Witchcraft?!

Many Christians unwittingly practice witchcraft through **The Spiritual Law of Agreement**. Does that sound strange? Such unsuspecting and presumptuous Christians are soul-driven and not Spirit-led. Consequently, they are prone to spiritual traps which the enemy uses.

Divination among soul-driven Christians occurs when two or three presumptuously gather in agreement to decree that which is not God's will. Satan then uses their words.

Witchcraft in the Bible is better translated as "divination". In this regard, divination is not the macabre scene of black hooded old women stirring pots of smoking potions as they cackle their chants.

Jay Adam Clark, a well-reputed expositor of the Bible, says:

> "Divination is the art of speaking secret knowledge, especially of the future or speaking under inspired satanic utterance, whether by voice or in written form. It is a pagan counterfeit of righteous prophecy. Careful comparison of Scripture will reveal that inspirational divination is by demonic power, whereas genuine prophecy is by the Spirit of God."

Confession forms the union of **agreement**, and **agreement** is the power of life. We see this principle in Jesus' own words:

> *"Again I say to you that if two of you **agree** on earth about anything that they may ask* [declare, confess, or request], *it shall be done for them by My Father who is in Heaven. 20 For where two or three have gathered together in My name, I am there in their midst." (Matthew 18:19-20. Square brackets added by author for clarity.)*

The power released by *agreement* and *confession* in the above Scripture is founded upon "**righteous agreement**". Jesus is in the

The Spiritual Laws of Communication, Agreement, Alignment, Confession, and Transfer

midst of them. Obviously, this implies they are in **agreement** with God's will, and not asserting their own will, or assuming something is God's will, when in fact it is contrary to God's will. For this reason, rightly dividing God's Word and being led by His Spirit is vital.

But what happens when Christians presumptuously **align** with a wrong spirit and by **agreement** speak **confessions** and declarations? Is it a holy gathering because they gather in the name of Jesus? What becomes of their words?

In such cases, Satan uses their declarations (**confessions**) to license demonic activity. This is why he waited for Balaam to speak curses over Israel.

When Christians gather in **agreement** contrary to God's will (whether they realize it or not), it is classic divination under the pretense of the Christian faith! Satan uses the same dynamic of spiritual laws where words are released as curses spoken by Christians who thought they were speaking by the Lord!

In George Otis Jr's book, The Twilight Labyrinth, he makes an astute observation and says, "But the hard fact is, human presumption is among the most common *attractors* to the demonic."[11]

It is critical, therefore, that we avoid presumption and act only by the leading of the Holy Spirit. We must verify our personal sense of justice by God's Spirit and seek His will.

Sometimes a Word from God is perplexing. This is especially true if it doesn't meet the standard of people's presumption. How surprising to them when they discover *it is a Word from the Lord*.

Sometimes what can appear as a Word from God, by presumption, is in fact a word of the enemy. This type of interplay was the mainstream of Jezebel. She spoke words that seemed to be God's Words.

---

[11] Otis, George Jr., The Twilight Labyrinth, Grand Rapids, MI, Baker House Company, 1998, page 246.

The Spiritual Laws of Communication, Agreement, Alignment, Confession, and Transfer

The same may be said of Peter's words to Jesus. Jesus immediately rebuked Satan's influence as spoken through Peter.

The standard for judging such words is how *perfectly* exact they interface with God's written Word *and* its context of use.

Again, consider the Christian man whom Paul handed over to Satan for the destruction of the flesh. Immature Christians gasp at such judgment. Initially, nothing about Paul's decision seemed consistent with God's love, mercy, and grace. But, in fact, it was a unique application of mercy to turn the man from the consequence of eternal damnation and rectify sin in the church. This is why we are admonished to "rightly" divide the Word of God (2 Timothy 2:15).

Consider the woman, Jezebel, in Revelation 2:20-23. John is commanded by Jesus to write a letter to the pastor of the church in Thyatira.

> *"But I have this against you that you tolerate the woman Jezebel, who calls herself a prophetess and she teaches and leads my bondservants astray so that they commit acts of immorality and eat things sacrificed to idols. 21 I gave her time to repent of her immorality. 22 Behold I will throw her onto a bed of sickness, <u>and those who commit adultery with her</u> into great tribulation, unless they repent of her deeds, 23 And I will kill her children with pestilence and all the churches will know that I am He who searches the minds and hearts; and I will give to each one according to your deeds."* (Underline by author for added emphasis.)

The immorality referred to in this passage is "spiritual immorality". Specifically, there was a faction within the church of Thyatira that spiritually **aligned** with Jezebel and her doctrines.

She was considered as a prophetess who was deeply spiritual and operated in spiritual gifts. She had the respect and devotion of many in the church. In brief, she was full of herself and had a following in the congregation.

The Spiritual Laws of Communication, Agreement, Alignment, Confession, and Transfer

Jesus warned the church and those who **aligned** with her about her doctrine. Because she was given time to repent, it suggests she was a Christian who strayed from the truth.

Imagine that John brings his letter to the congregation. As he stands before the church, he calls out the woman that claimed to be a prophetess. She is highly respected. Many believe her to be spiritually wise, influential, and accurate in the things she says.

John asks her to stand up. Then he says, "God has given you time to repent and you would not. Therefore, He is casting you onto a bed of sickness. Furthermore, those who are **aligned** with you will experience great trouble in their lives unless they disavow your influence in their lives and repent."

The congregation gasps in shock. This woman has an impressive spiritual reputation. She has favor and influence in the church. Many received words from her and considered her an admirable Christian. How could John say such things?

Let's take this to the next step: She stands silently offended. She is humiliated by the rebuke and seething in anger. After John is finished, she sits down.

Immediately after the service, she plays the role of a martyr and gathers her entourage of friends and sympathizers. She has no spiritual comprehension that John's rebuke came from Jesus.

Reproved for her sins, she goes about the church secretly campaigning from person to person. She **communicates** with various "select" members—her sympathizers. They are surprised, even offended that John, who obviously does not know this woman, would say such things. None of his words matched the woman's credibility.

At her house, she meets with faithful supporters and holds a special prayer meeting. In patriotic zeal, those **aligned** with her are equally offended. They gather in Jesus' name to denounce, decree, declare, rebuke, and bind. With great zeal, they command John's words to

The Spiritual Laws of Communication, Agreement, Alignment, Confession, and Transfer

be of no effect. They praise Jesus who paid for their sicknesses and washed away their sins. They assure one another that Jesus would never cast anyone onto a bed of sickness (1 Peter 2:24). They are confident that He would never trouble the lives of her followers—after all, they love Jesus and Jesus loves them. Did not Jesus say that in this world there will be tribulations, and that they were to take joy because Jesus overcame the world (John 16:33)?

John's words do not meet their standard of God's love. Consequently, they denounce his words, label them as false, and designate them as being sent from the spirit of darkness.

Having gathered together in Jesus' name, they bind John's decree, which they claim is a demonically inspired judgment (Matthew 18:20). They comfort their prophetess and promise her that the Lord will cover and protect her.

Time proves all things.

Soon, Jezebel complains about not feeling well. Her entourage gathers around her, anoints her with oil, and rebukes the words of divination and witchcraft that John spoke over her life. But nothing changes. She gets worse, and in time, she dies. John is then blamed for cursing her.

Soon thereafter, her followers are plagued with various troubles: financial issues, relationships, sickness, loss of jobs, problems with children, and a plethora of other entanglements that intersect their lives. Nothing seems to work; peace is removed. Their alliance, one with another, crumbles and they scatter. Blinded by arrogance and pride, and because of their **agreement** and **alignment** with the prophetess, they failed to correlate God's sword set against them. Somehow the warning Jesus gave them escapes their understanding.

There is no lasting unity in anything Satan organizes. By nature, he is divisive, destructive, and self-serving. On many occasions I have seen this drama play itself out in the lives of Christians, especially by those that cause division in a church. Their dark satanic

The Spiritual Laws of Communication, Agreement, Alignment, Confession, and Transfer

agreement that binds them together soon loses strength. Their cohesiveness quickly dissolves after Satan is finished with them. Do a longevity study and track their outcomes. In every case they are disconnected, wandering, and disoriented.

Most of the time, God's sword of penalty does not instantly manifest. But know this for certain: when the violation against God's spiritual laws occur, the action of His sword immediately begins even if it is not apparent or obvious.

"Yet, wisdom is vindicated by all her children." (Luke 7:35)

God's Word is always proven by results. His wisdom never fails.

STORY: My wife and I were members of a church in which the pastor separated himself from a well-respected denomination. Incrementally, he drifted by degrees from the truth until his works could fittingly be called cultic.

Being troubled in my spirit and an elder in the church, I called the pastor and met with him to discuss the issues. He was politely resistant to the truth. In time, I had no choice but to leave the church after doing all that the Lord required of me.

Because I did not want wrong seeds planted in the future of my ministry, I carefully considered the Scriptural way to leave. I refrained from speaking to anyone about the pastor or influencing anyone in the church to follow me. The Lord would show them the error, just as He did for me.

When people complained to me about him, I immediately cut off the conversation and told them they needed to go to him in private, not me. I refused to be used in sedition against his church, him, or his ministry. He was the Lord's servant, not mine. God would deal with him.

Within the same year after leaving the church, we moved forward in ministry. I was appointed as the Executive Vice President of a

The Spiritual Laws of Communication, Agreement, Alignment, Confession, and Transfer

well-known international ministry several states away. Then strange events started happening.

During the first year after leaving the church, Satan made two distinct attempts against my daughter's life by drowning. She was just under three years of age at the time.

In the first attempt, Sarah was next to me within about ten inches of my right arm and we were watching minnows in a large muddy-water pond in the park. The pond had a cement curbing around it. I was tossing bread crumbs on the water and minnows sporadically came to the surface to eat.

I asked Sarah if she wanted to hold a minnow. She eagerly agreed. My intention was to splash the water's surface and hopefully send a minnow onto the grass.

I was poised and ready to slap the water when something directly in front of me about two feet away caught my eye. What I saw was Sarah's hand go under the water as she reached upward to the surface! She made no splash entering the water. Nor did I see the mass of her body move from my peripheral view to a position directly in front of me only inches away!

It was impossible for her to enter the water without making a noticeable splash. What happened was nothing less than supernatural—a genuine demonic attack.

I blindly reached into the muddy-colored water, grabbed for any part of her body, and lifted her out of the pond into my arms. My wife, standing directly to my left side, never saw her enter the water. How was any of that possible within a less than three-foot circle?

About six months later, Sarah and I were standing on the five-foot wide walkway of a boat pier in Lake Meade, Nevada. When I looked down to my left side, she was about five feet under the surface of the crystal clear water that was some forty-feet deep. I dove into the lake and saved her. Once we were safely back on the dock, I asked how she fell in and she said someone pushed her. There was

The Spiritual Laws of Communication, Agreement, Alignment, Confession, and Transfer

no one around us. Again, there was no splash of water when she went in.

A few months later, I was talking to a friend of mine that formerly attended the church we had left. He told me the pastor spoke a declaration to the congregation against my daughter's life by saying that God would take Sarah from me because I loved her more than God.

According to him, I was in the sin of idolatry. Members of the congregation quickly **agreed** with him. It was not true, of course, but the congregation patriotically **aligned** with him on anything he said. Through divination by their power of **agreement** and **alignment**, a hideous spirit of murder was released against my daughter.

During the conversation with my friend, the Lord showed me that the pastor spoke a curse over her life. I stopped immediately and commanded it to be broken. After that, there was never another incident.

Here was a Christian man, a pastor, that departed from the accurate handling of God's Word and satanically spoke a decree based on his personal disdain. His decree was presented as if it was a judgment from God. Added to that, members of his church **aligned** with his words, **agreed** with them, **confessed** them, and licensed the demonic activity.

Once the divination was discovered, I commanded it to be annulled by the authority of the Lord Jesus. In this case, the spiritual harassment had to be dealt with. The pastor's dark words, spoken by the inspiration of a dark spirit, were licensed in the realm of the demonic and sent against me and my daughter. Astounding to many, they thought he spoke by the Holy Spirit's inspiration under a righteous pretense—groundless as it was.

★★★

Can Christians annul any decree they choose by invoking the name of Jesus? Absolutely not! Specific to certain spiritual laws, there are penalties of God that carry heavy swords. Disregarding this fact,

The Spiritual Laws of Communication, Agreement, Alignment, Confession, and Transfer

carnal Christians babble their superficial religious decrees termed as "spiritual warfare". They denounce, rebuke, bind, and declare—all with no power in what they say. They work-up religious fervor and think they are tearing down strongholds. It is all of the flesh. Their words carry no weight against God's righteousness. Unwittingly, they enter into divination and have no clue that they vainly speak against the very judgments of God.

The penalties of God's spiritual laws cannot be rebuked. His Word cannot be altered. There is no power that can stand against them. His Kingdom is unshakable, and the gates of hell cannot prevail against God's authority.

The spiritual force of God's sword is actively against those who practice evil (Romans 13:4). Until they repent, no amount of fervent vociferous decrees, prayers, chanting, declarations, rebukes, binding and loosening, fasting, anointing with oil, or any type of religious exercise can stop the sword. God's laws are subject only to Himself.

Consequently, when a person is warned by the Holy Spirit to turn from darkness and they refuse to listen, or if they renounce His warning, then God's mercy ends and His judgments begin.

STORY: An attractive woman in my church had great zest in all that she endeavored. She had just gotten her realtor's license in a ski resort town where property values were exceedingly high. In fact, many of the Hollywood A-listers lived there.

A world-renown prophet, Dick Mills, came to my church. When he was ministering, he cordially pointed to the woman and asked her to stand up. He started with, "I am hesitant to give this word simply because it is rare in the Body of Christ. But I am going to be obedient and tell you. What you do with it is up to you: God has given you a ministry like Kathryn Kuhlman. You will fill ballrooms, meeting halls, and large places where people will come to hear you. Signs and wonders will follow you. Again, it is up to you what you do with that word."

The Spiritual Laws of Communication, Agreement, Alignment, Confession, and Transfer

People in the congregation were in awe. This prophet (whom I knew personally) walked with deep integrity more than anyone I have ever met. His words were accurate and incredibly revealing in the Lord. The fruits of the Holy Spirit in his life were as equally strong as the gifts of the Holy Spirit.

Sadly, the woman never entered the calling. Instead, she grew enamored with her realty success and focused on her business. When it came to real estate sales in the region, she was a household name. She acquired properties, rentals, made a middle six-figure income, and owned nice cars.

Years later, I moved to a distant city. The Lord quickened me to remind her of the calling He placed on her life. I wrote a letter and told her this was her last chance; that by now she would have been known throughout the world; and that she would be lacking nothing.

She replied with an angry condescending letter and spurned the Lord's last offer. In fact, within a few years, she was known as the town lush. She lost her popularity as a dependable realtor and slipped into a lifestyle of gross sexual revelry. Even her children were uncomfortable with her being around the grandchildren. She never entered the ministry. Instead, she remained deeply saturated in the world.

She retained an *academic* knowledge of the Kingdom and spoke in spiritual terms in the company of Christians. Even then, however, her frequent unguarded profanity revealed the depth of her relationship with the Lord.

It was sad. Like Judas, who was given an eternal honor among the Apostles, she threw it all away for money.

> "For rebellion is as the sin of divination, and insubordination is as iniquity and idolatry." *(1 Samuel 15:23)*

★ ★ ★

The Spiritual Laws of Communication, Agreement, Alignment, Confession, and Transfer

The Spiritual Laws of Transfer and Alignment

Communication *precedes* **agreement**; **agreement** *precedes* **alignment**; **alignment** *precedes* **confession**; **confession** *precedes* **transfer**. **Transfer** is the final stage.

Agreement can come in the form of action including words. For example, when a message is given in church, the pastor or speaker might give an altar call. Coming forward is a response to **agreement**. Getting out of the chair, coming forward as a testimony in front of everyone is a catalyst that activates **The Spiritual Law of Alignment**. It is a wordless **alignment** by **agreement**.

Water baptism, a command of Jesus Christ, is a physical demonstration that acknowledges all He did for our salvation. In **agreement**, we proclaim His death, burial, and resurrection through the formality of water baptism. Water baptism is a catalyst that changes one's testimony from the ethereal to the literal.

When Jesus was crucified, we were in Him. And when He rose from the dead, we arose with Him in the newness of life (Romans 6). The water signifies the death and the washing away of our sins. When we come up out of the water, it represents the resurrection and the newness of life in Jesus. We are **aligned** with Jesus because we first **agree** with the **communicated** Gospel that we **confess**. His righteousness is then **transferred** to us by truth and sealed by the Holy Spirit.

EXAMPLES: In the proper sequence of these five interconnecting spiritual laws, **transfer** is the fifth and final step of the process. Once the **transfer** is complete, the individual is laminated to whatever he or she is **aligned** with through **agreement** according to their words (**confession**).

Agreement does not of itself have to be a spoken official decree or writ of declaration. Rather, it can be shared sentiments expressed in various conversations, rumors, gossip, and through different stages or collections of conversations. We often enter **agreement** without

The Spiritual Laws of Communication, Agreement, Alignment, Confession, and Transfer

realizing our words and actions and how they bind us to the outcome.

We see these spiritual laws when Judas stubbornly set his heart to betray Jesus. After Satan entered him, Jesus told Judas to quickly do what he planned (Luke 22:3). The **transfer** was complete and Judas' was given over to his sin. When Judas fell, it was not suddenly. He fell systematically in stages and degrees. Before his fall, he entered into **agreement** with the Pharisees to betray Jesus.

Korah, Dathan, and Abiram were three men that opposed Moses in which, again, we see the same spiritual laws of **communication, agreement, alignment, confession, and transfer.**

Korah was the leader of three malcontents which included himself along with Dathan and Abiram.

In every group of dissenters, there is always a lead-voice, Satan's ambassador which he uses as a spokesperson—the ringleader.

Typically, when dissenters gather, they **align** by a mutually shared sentiments—a rallying point which is the working of a critical and or cynical spirit—a form of **communication**. By **agreement** they form **alignment**s. In this case, Korah was the lead voice and they were tired of roaming the desert—as was everyone else. Using this common point of disdain, they came together by **communication** in order to form **agreements**.

If they were to overthrow Moses, they needed more persuasion and power than just the three of them. Consequently, they spent a great deal of time campaigning among the Israelites and rounding up leaders. Ultimately, from among the three-million-person congregation, two hundred fifty renown men were "chosen" by the assembly.

This took a considerable amount of time to organize, perhaps weeks of diligence with many meetings. As it might have seemed, mysteriously, a plague of sedition silently moved among the congregation. Meanwhile, God watched. Nothing is hidden from Him.

The Spiritual Laws of Communication, Agreement, Alignment, Confession, and Transfer

He heard their murmurings (**communications**) and accusations. He watched their agreements form. He saw their **alignments** coming together and knew the motivation of their hearts. He watched as the storm gathered momentum. And, He knew the end-result of their troublemaking.

Moses, however, had no idea that a coup was developing. In fact, by God's own words, Moses was the most humble man on the earth (Numbers 12:3).

As the number of rebels increased, the fifth step in the sequence of "**transfer**" solidified their bond. They were now given over to their sin. The outcome was set—an ending disaster of which they had no comprehension. Again, we saw this same sequence in Judas' life.

The same pattern happens in church splits. It is never sudden. It is always a stealthy developing **alignment** of malcontents subversively working by casual conversation (**communication**), testing reactions of possible candidates, and selectively recruiting weak people.

The strong ones are never duped into such foolery. Typically, they are never approached. As if led by a dark spirit, malcontents intuitively know who to approach—the weak and shallow ones.

Murmuring is the connecting thread that invigorates their complaints and fuels the discord. This is their **communication**. **Agreement** is their strength. **Alignment** is their purpose. **Confession** is their union. **Transfer** solidifies their spiritual bond one to the other, and they are given over to their sin. Individually, they are cowards, but in numbers, they are confident.

Complaining is the connecting thread of murmurers. Agreement is their mutual strength. Alignment is their purpose. Confession is their union, and transfer is their solidarity.

The Spiritual Laws of Communication, Agreement, Alignment, Confession, and Transfer

Moses' tribe, the Levites, was Korah's family tribe. Korah's hidden motivation was to have preeminence so that he could rule the people (Numbers 16:6-10). He touted himself and all the people as being no different than Moses (Numbers 16:3).

Nothing could be more convincing, brazen, or emblematic than for Moses' family tribe to oppose him in an open public display.

As the process continued, the Lord watched. Every word, every action, every plan, and every part was recorded in Heaven. He listened to their words spoken in secret. He watched their clandestine meetings. He listened as they chewed up Moses' character. He waited and gave them time to repent. But when their cup overflowed, the sword would strike.

Korah and his two hundred fifty leaders, along with various numbers of the congregation confidently organized a public showdown and confronted Moses. The line was drawn. Being laminated to their sin, they were spiritually blind and overwhelmingly arrogant.

Moses set forth a public test in the Lord. The next day, Korah and his mob were to bring their censers, put fire in them from the brazen altar, and lay incense upon them in the presence of the Lord.

This specific incense was a special mixture that no one was allowed to possess except the Levite priests (Exodus 30:34-37). The burning fragrance represented holy prayers offered to the Lord. When it was burned, the man whom the Lord chose would be holy—separated unto Him.

Meanwhile, Moses sent messengers asking for Dathan and Abiram to meet with him. They refused and condescendingly sent a messenger to Moses saying, *"Is it not enough that you have brought us up out of a land flowing with milk and honey [this was the oppressive slavery of Egypt,], to have us die in the wilderness, but you would also lord it over us."* (Numbers 16:13. *Square brackets added by author for clarity.)*

The Spiritual Laws of Communication, Agreement, Alignment, Confession, and Transfer

Moses knew God's fury was churning. The Bible says that Moses knew the "ways" of God, but the people only understood the "acts" of God (Psalms 103:7).

When sedition finds its way into a church, the Lord will show the pastor the sword that befalls those who trouble God's house.

Creating schism and division in God's house ranks among the worst of sins. It is the one sin that tells us to mark those who cause division among the saints. This type of division ranks just below the three unforgiveable sins: blasphemy of the Holy Spirit (Mark 3:29); receiving the Mark of the Beast (Revelation 14:9), and the sin unto death (Hebrews 6:4-6; 1 John 5:16).

> *"Now I urge you, brethren, note those who cause divisions and offenses, contrary to the doctrine which you learned, and avoid them." (Romans 16:17)*

Korah and his entourage presumed themselves to be righteous. In blind haughty pride, they expected God to stand with them against His favored servant, Moses. It was a deadly contest.

When the sword falls, sometimes the consequence is unimaginable. In this case, death was the penalty.

The audacity and presumption of Korah, Dathan, and Abiram, along with the two hundred fifty chosen renown leaders, confronted God's chosen leader, Moses, at the doorway of the Tent of Meeting. This was the sacred place where God came down from Heaven and met with Moses face-to-face (Numbers 12:1-2-4-16).

With the crowd gathered against him, the Lord's anger burned hot. He wanted to consume the entire congregation of three million people and destroy them in an instant. This was because the entire congregation was aligned with Korah's position. They were infected with the spirit of sedition. Moses, however, interceded and asked God to deal only with the malcontents. As a result, the Lord opened the earth and swallowed the men, their families, their little ones, and all their possessions. After that, fire came down from Heaven.

The Spiritual Laws of Communication, Agreement, Alignment, Confession, and Transfer

In a moment, the two hundred fifty renowned leaders that offered "strange incense" were turned into sudden ash (Numbers 16:28-35).

Their prayers, words, complaints, murmurings, and criticisms came before God as intolerable filth. They had violated God's appointed servant and showed no regard for the Lord's choosing.

★★★

In this tragic display of arrogance, pride, and presumption that resulted in a mass judgment, critically important observations need to be noted.

God lists seven deadly sins as warnings for us, the same sins that Korah and his rebels committed against God's chosen servant:

> *"There are six things the Lord hates, seven that are detestable to Him: 17 haughty eyes, 16 a lying tongue, hands that shed innocent blood, 18 a heart that devises wicked scheme, feet that are quick to rush to evil, 19 a false witness who pours out lies and a person who stirs up conflict in the community."*
> *(Proverbs 6:16-19)*

1. *Haughty eyes:* Eyes are the windows to the soul. Whatever is in the heart, whether words or actions, will manifest in one's life. This is the summary **confession** of their mouth. A person with haughty eyes has a prideful heart. Such people are conceited, self-serving, and have no regard for others or the damages they inflict by their hidden agendas. Above all, they are the most dangerous people. They live only for themselves without any concern for how their decisions affect others.

2. *A lying tongue:* This was laughable. They called Egypt the land flowing with milk and honey. In fact, they were in cruel servitude. A critical spirit and deception always work in union with exaggerations. *Truth* is expendable and least of all valued.

3. *Hands that shed innocent blood:* This is both literal and figurative. People who attack another person's life in the form of hateful words, lies, accusations, and judgments are spiritual felons. Without

The Spiritual Laws of Communication, Agreement, Alignment, Confession, and Transfer

conscience, they shed innocent blood by attacking the life of another. Seldom do such hateful people comprehend the collateral damage they cause which later manifests in their own life. In 1 John 3:15, it says that whoever hates his brother is a murderer. Metaphorically, they shed blood. Moses was hated by Korah. If Korah had prevailed, his mob would have killed Moses and Israel would have been devoured without God's covering.

4. *A heart that devises wicked things.* The presumptuous sin of Korah and his mutineers had no respect for God nor God's choosing of Moses. Audaciously, they superimposed their own leadership. Because their canopy and covering would have been removed, had they succeeded it would have ended in the total annihilation of the Israelites. In their presumption, God was not obligated to honor their leaders simply because He did not choose them. They were Satan's elect.

5. *Feet that rush to evil.* Korah's campaign among the congregation was a long-drawn-out process. It was something he and his men seditiously relished as they moved in stealth throughout the people.

6. *A false witness who pours out lies.* Half-truths, slanted facts, out of context quotes, and the intentional design of deception is the craft of people bonded in unrighteousness. Truth is *never* valued among such complainers. The divination that binds one to the other is a storm that gathers energy. What they never consider, however, is the sword that follows. For Korah and his mob, it was death.

7. *And a person who stirs up conflict in the community.* These are those, who *selectively* seek counsel to bring people into **agreement** (which is never godly counsel), but rather bias **agreement**. Under the disguise of seeking counsel, they are actually gossips (**communicators**) with a seditious spirit of vengeance. Their angle of approach is hidden with religious fronts. Inwardly, their real motivation is deceit and a self-serving agenda. Korah and his group showed no regard for the Lord, the Lord's house, or the potential disaster of destroying the Israelites if they had prevailed.

The Spiritual Laws of Communication, Agreement, Alignment, Confession, and Transfer

If this scenario happened in a modern church, consider the network of spiritual laws that are violated. In Matthew 18:15, Korah should have spoken to Moses in private. However, Korah had no heart for righteousness. He subversively worked behind the scene and **communicated** his sinister plan to select others with the baleful intention of recruitment. This enacted the first step: **The Spiritual Law of Communication**.

In the second step, Korah mustered those that **agreed** with him. By **The Spiritual Law of Agreement**, he gathered a core-entourage of followers that bonded with his complaint.

In the third step, **The Spiritual Law of Alignment** was centered upon a mutual complaint of roaming in the desert too long. This is where the spirit of criticism arose by using every fragment of discord and disdain that could be mustered.

In the fourth step, they united as one voice and one objective by **The Spiritual Law of Confession**.

Finally, in the fifth step, everyone was bound over to darkness by **The Spiritual Law of Transfer**. Once the **transfer** was complete, the force of destruction was assembled.

Satan's Real Motivation

Korah and his cronies showed no consideration for the Lord's chosen people through which the Messiah would ultimately come as Savior of the world. Consequently, when Korah launched his heinous plan against Moses, he ignorantly but recklessly attacked God's plan for the salvation of mankind. The Jews are the chosen people through which salvation came to the world, namely that of Jesus Christ through the tribe of Judah.

Satan could see God's plan, but he needed someone like Korah to dismantle it. Korah planted mutinous seeds throughout the three-million-congregation. For this reason, God demonstrated His judgment for all to see. He wanted every person to know that Moses was His chosen servant.

The Spiritual Laws of Communication, Agreement, Alignment, Confession, and Transfer

The same laws of **communication**, **agreement**, **alignment**, **confession**, **and transfer** are equally powerful in righteousness.

We see this in Jesus' Apostles and the Seventy (Luke 10:1). Jesus *communicated* the Gospel to them; they stood in *agreement*; *aligned* in common cause; *confessed* their union of purpose; and He *transferred* His anointing upon them. Every step was essential.

> *"The seventy returned with joy saying, "Lord even the demons are subject to us in Your name." 18 And He said to them, I was watching Satan fall from Heaven like lightening. 19 Behold I have given you authority to tread upon serpents and scorpions, and over all the power of the enemy, and nothing will harm you." (Luke 10:17-19)*

The Spiritual Law of Pairing

Anointings enhance between people according to **The Spiritual Law of Pairing**. I have seen this dynamic occur over and over. The strength of one person's gift influences the strength of another's person's gift. For example, when God initially endows a person with the gift of prophecy, He pairs them with experienced prophets. The gifting of the lesser is enhanced by the anointing of the greater.

Through **The Spiritual Law of Pairing,** God divinely appoints relationships. In this manner, impartations come by close association one to the other—not necessarily through the laying on of hands. The process is through **communication**, **agreement**, **alignment**, **confession**, and **transfer**.

We see this model with Paul and Timothy; Titus, and Silvanus; Paul with Luke; Moses with Joshua; Moses and the Seventy Judges; Elisha with Elijah; and Jesus with the eleven apostles, to name just a few.

Sadly, many fail to recognize God's arrangement of Divine Relationships. However, Satan *does* recognize them! He understands the exponential power that comes through divine pairing and the strength it produces. Therefore, he targets such relationships before they reach effective synergistic levels of power. Take special care,

The Spiritual Laws of Communication, Agreement, Alignment, Confession, and Transfer

therefore, to guard, keep, and preserve them. Every divinely appointed relationship will be tested and forged by fire.

If divinely appointed relationships of God are devalued, He is not obligated to replace them. Consequently, without divine pairing, one's journey is difficult, slow, and limited. We see this model with Apollos, an eloquent and powerful speaker. Initially, He lacked mentorship. But after he was mentored, his ministry exponentially increased.

> *"Now a Jew named Apollos, an Alexandrian by birth, an eloquent man, came to Ephesus; and he was mighty in the Scriptures. 25 This man had been instructed in the way of the Lord; and being fervent in spirit, he was speaking and teaching accurately the things concerning Jesus, [but] being acquainted only with the baptism of John; 26 and he began to speak out boldly in the synagogue. But when Priscilla and Aquila* [a husband and wife team] *heard him, they took him aside and explained to him the way of God more accurately [by instructing him in the full revelation of salvation through Jesus]." (Acts 18:23-26. Square brackets by author for added clarity.)*

What if Apollos had failed to value the mentorship offered him? The limitations within his ministry would have been a slow progress in discovering the truth. Conversely, how long would it be until someone came along that supplemented his anointing and calling?

When God ordains pairing, He joins compatible callings and anointings. He enhances the lesser by the greater in order to raise the lesser to a greater level. For example, the Lord does not typically pair the office of the pastor with the office of evangelist. Such offices are mismatched in their general design. The pastor's office is mostly non-traveling; the evangelist's office is continual traveling. The wisdom of the pastor's office that operates within the local church is different than the wisdom of the evangelist's office that operates in the general sense of the Body of Christ universally.

The great Kathryn Kuhlman's ministry was filled with signs, wonders, and miracles. She openly confessed that she was not God's first

The Spiritual Laws of Communication, Agreement, Alignment, Confession, and Transfer

choice, but instead, God's third choice. The first two individuals, whoever they were, did not respond to the Lord's calling.

When complimentary anointings come together, the synergistic effect is exponential power. The same dynamic applies to those who **align** with others against God's spiritual laws. Their exponential destruction produces a sword against them. In some cases, such as with Korah, Dathan, and Abiram, it is lethal,.

Chapter Eight
The Spiritual Law of Confession and The Spiritual Law of Dignitary Authority

"But if her father refuses to let her make the vow or feels that the penalties she has agreed to are too harsh, then her promise will automatically become invalid. Her father must state his disagreement on the first day he hears about it, and then Jehovah will forgive her because her father would not let her do it." (Numbers 30:5)

STORY: A particular woman in church was diagnosed with a progressive disease. The church anointed her with oil and kept her before the Lord with intercessory prayer. In addition to her church attendance, at various times she and her husband received home visits for prayer to encourage them in God's promises of healing.

Her Christian husband, however, came from a mainline denomination and was never taught about God's healing promises. In fact, he had never seen a miracle. Nonetheless, he believed God healed people on *rare* occasions.

Even though the woman was firm and positive in her faith, she slowly digressed in health. Since the faith of so many that prayed for her

The Spiritual Law of Confession and the Spiritual Law of Dignitary Authority

was strong and resolute, it was perplexing as to why she did not improve.

Everyone could see her husband's tender love, patience, and care as he attended to her every need. Nonetheless, hidden spiritual laws were set into motion that countered the prayers being offered.

Being the priest and husband of his household, he stood in the position of **Dignitary Authority**. He had no understanding of the power he possessed by God's design of marriage. Without knowing it, he voided the prayers offered for her healing by strong unbelief. Each time after she was prayed for, when everyone left their house, he privately asked her how she wanted the funeral conducted; where she wanted her ashes spread; and what to do with certain articles of her possessions. He made no provision for her healing, but instead planned for her death in complete disregard for her healing or the prayers offered to the Lord.

When it was told that they should change the atmosphere of their home with continual songs of worship and praises to the Lord—songs that honored His presence, he refused any such activity. He rather preferred the house to be quiet and still.

Much to the grief of her family and friends, eventually the woman died.

What happened is this case? According to God's design in the government of marriage, the husband stood in **Dignitary Authority** over the domain of his household. This included his wife. But he walked in fear, doubt, unbelief, and continually confessed her death as an outcome. As the priest of his home and by the words he used, he annulled the prayers of faith over her life. This was not his intention. He had no idea he was doing this. Nonetheless, by his authority, he unwittingly set spiritual laws into motion of which he was completely ignorant. His words and belief aligned with death.

★★★

Just as faith is a powerful force, unbelief is a powerful force. For this reason, when Jesus raised Jairus' daughter from the dead, the first

The Spiritual Law of Confession and the Spiritual Law of Dignitary Authority

thing He did was command all the doubters and unbelievers to leave the room in order to construct an atmosphere of solidarity in faith. He did not want their aggressive unbelief conflicting with the operation of His faith. By this, Jesus applied **The Spiritual Laws of Agreement, Alignment, Confession,** and **Dignitary Authority** when He performed certain miracles (Luke 8:51-56).

After Jesus removed the doubters, only Peter, James, John, and the child's parents were allowed to remain. The child's parents stood in **Dignitary Authority** over the child while Peter, James, and John stood with Jesus in **the power of agreement**.

Some assume that Jesus does not require the power of agreement to work miracles. At times, depending on the situation, that was true. However, when He returned to His hometown of Nazareth, the villagers took exception to Him. They knew His family and perceived Him as nothing more than the former town carpenter.

> *"Coming to his hometown, he began teaching the people in their synagogue, and they were amazed. "Where did this man get this wisdom and these miraculous powers?" they asked. 55 "Isn't this the carpenter's son? Isn't His mother's name Mary, and aren't His brothers James, Joseph, Simon, and Judas? 56 Aren't all His sisters with us? Where then did this man get all these things?" 57 And they took offense at Him. But Jesus said to them, "A prophet is not without honor except in his own town and in his own home." 58 And He did not do many miracles there because of their lack of faith."* (Matthew 13:54-58)

In this instance, their agreement and alignment with unbelief prevented them from receiving Jesus' anointing. Yet, by comparison, when Jesus ministered in Capernaum (Matthew 8:14-17), the town exploded in miracles, salvations, and deliverances.

Agreement and confession are powerful forces that work with faith. In the same way, agreement and confession is a powerful force that works with unbelief.

The Spiritual Law of Confession and the Spiritual Law of Dignitary Authority

The Spiritual Law of Dignitary Authority has great power and preference before the Lord, but it also comes with great responsibility.

When blind Bartimaeus called out to Jesus, they brought him through the crowd to the Lord. Jesus asked him what he wanted. It was obvious, wasn't it? He wanted to see again. The purpose of Jesus asking the question was to bring Bartimaeus' faith into agreement with the faith of Jesus. By Bartimaeus speaking his request, **The Spiritual Law of Agreement** came into play (Mark 10:46-52).

This, of course, takes nothing from the Lord's sovereignty to do as He pleases. He performed many miracles without asking for agreement. In one such miracle, He stopped a funeral procession in Nain, spoke to the dead body, and raised the man back to life (Luke 17:11-17). In that case, however, the *active force of a pre-set unbelief* was not present as it was in His hometown of Nazareth.

While **The Spiritual Law of Dignitary Authority** holds great power and preference before the Lord, it also comes with great responsibility. Eli had authority as a priest and a father to deal with his son's sins. Yet, in complacency and apathy, he let them do as they wanted. As a consequence, the sword came into play and the Lord said there would never be an acceptable sacrifice for the house of Eli forever.

> *"Honor your father and mother, as the lord your God has commanded you, that your days may be prolonged and that it may go well with you on the land which the Lord your God gives you."*
> *(Deuteronomy 5:16)*

As long as the parents of children are alive during the life of the children, this command remains perpetually in force. It is the only commandment of the Ten Commandments that comes with a promise. At the same time, **The Spiritual Law of Implied Reverse** carries a sword if the parent(s) are dishonored. Consequently, it will NOT go well with the children. The command is not based on the parent's

The Spiritual Law of Confession and the Spiritual Law of Dignitary Authority

perfection; it is based on the parent's position of Dignitary Authority. God's demands that it be respected.

God gives parents Dignitary Authority because He commands them to raise their children in the admonition of His Word. Therefore, because He holds the parents accountable, when they pray for their children, He regards their prayer. In this consideration, parents have preference before the Lord as they petition God for help whenever they pray for their children, be they adults or minors.

Parents stand in Dignitary Authority because they are commanded by the Lord to raise their children in the admonition of God's righteousness.

Pastors stand in Dignitary Authority because the Lord holds them responsible for those to whom they minister. If a pastor allows error in the church and does not correct the doctrine, God will discipline the pastor. At the same time, if the pastor is faithful before the Lord and stands watchful and caring over the people, then the Lord will deal with the people. Because of this, God issues very stern Words:

> "Obey your leaders and submit to them, for they keep watch over your souls as those who will give an account. Let them do this with joy and not grief, for this would be unprofitable for you." *(Hebrews 13:17)*

People in Dignitary Authority must be careful what they decree and proclaim. Words, issued from the seat of their authority, carry power!

> "Death and life are in the power of the tongue and those who love it will eat its fruit." *(Proverbs 18:21)*

> "For by your words you will be justified, and by your words you will be condemned." *(Matthew 12:37)*

> "The tongue is a fire, the very world of iniquity; the tongue is set among our members as that which defiles the entire body, <u>and</u>

The Spiritual Law of Confession and the Spiritual Law of Dignitary Authority

<u>sets on fire the course of our life, and is set on fire by hell</u>." *(James 3:6. Underline by author for added emphasis.)*

Some people assume that **The Spiritual Law of Confession** can be manipulated for lustful gain. This law, however, does not work with self-indulgence. It is a law that works powerfully in righteousness according to God's will.

If our confessions can work against us in unbelief, then much more will our confessions work for us when we speak by God's oracles of faith!

If our unrighteous confessions work against us, then our righteous confessions will work for us! Kingdom-minded people are consciously aware of this truth. Regardless of the natural world around them, their speech reflects what they believe according to His promises.

People that deal with ongoing health issues often grow weary and less guarded over their soul. As a result, they lose vigilance and speak words of unbelief—even curses such as, "I can't do this anymore!", or "I just wish I could die and get it over with.", or "This is going to kill me."

Their confession speaks the *facts* about their condition while ignoring the superintending *truths* of God's promises. Before long, their words agree with defeat rather than the truths of God that bring victory.

A person might inform a close friend or family about the doctor's *factual* diagnosis. However, that is not necessarily the truth. The truth is what God says about the facts:

> "Bless the Lord O my soul, and forget none of His benefits, *3* who pardons all your iniquities, who heals all your diseases; *4* who redeems your life from the pit, who crowns you with lovingkindness and compassion, *5* who satisfies your life with good things so that your youth is renewed like the eagle." *(Pslam 103:2-5)*

The Spiritual Law of Confession and the Spiritual Law of Dignitary Authority

The word "confess" in the Greek is the word "homologeo" which means to say the same thing. It also means to agree with and declare according to that which is established.

Worshipping God, for instance, is the practice of homologeo—it is what we say, declare, proclaim, or sing about Him—a confession of what God reveals about Himself concerning His glory, power, love, attributes, and wisdom.

When God's Word is communicated to our spirit by God's Spirit, we come into agreement with His truth. We align with His truth in every point and castoff all unbelief. By confession, we say the same thing God says about the situation. This facilitates the transference of power. We take His truths, weave them into our lives, practice them, and receive His promises. Most of the time it works as a process and is not instant like a miracle.

Abraham, against natural hope at the age of one hundred years, believed God's Word to have a son with Sarah who was ninety years of age. For twenty-five years, Abraham believed without wavering, even in the face of increasing impossibility. Despite the natural reasons why it could not happen, Abraham agreed with God's Word that was communicated to him. He stayed in alignment with the promise. The Lord ascribed this to him as "righteousness".

The Spiritual Law of Confession works the same way when spoken words originate from the domain of darkness. Satan uses the law of declaration as a license for his works.

STORY: While in college, a Spirit-filled Christian friend took a strong interest in a beautiful young Mormon lady. I explained to him about **The Spiritual Law of Pairing** and pointed out that she was not a Christian; that he should not seek her company nor align with her; and that God's Word forbids any yoking in such relationships because she was not a Christian.

The Spiritual Law of Confession and the Spiritual Law of Dignitary Authority

I explained how Mormons believe that Jesus is a created being, not the Creator, and that He is the spirit-brother of Lucifer (Satan).[12]

My friend dismissed these warnings. Using self-serving excuses, he claimed he wanted to win her to Christ. I refuted this by saying the Lord would not honor his efforts because his motives were not genuine but rather self-serving.

I came home from classes one evening and discovered my roommate had invited two Mormon Missionaries to share their systematic well-rehearsed presentation of the Mormon religion. I sat down with them and changed the subject from their church doctrines to Jesus. I asked if they believed Jesus was the Creator—not someone who was created. Their answers were canned responses based on their training. In their belief, to them, Jesus was a created being. I refuted this with Scriptural examples but it made no difference.

After they left, I confronted my friend about having them at the house. He assured me that his reasons were to understand what they believed so that he could better witness to his hopeful romance.

> *"If anyone comes to you and does not bring this teaching [but diminishes or adds to the doctrine of Christ], do not receive or welcome him into your house, and do not give him a greeting or any encouragement." (2 John 1:10. Square brackets by author for added clarity.)*

Ignoring all warnings, my friend persisted in seeing the Mormon woman. He violated **The Spiritual Law of the Canopy** and stepped

---

[12] "[According to Mormon doctrine] On first hearing, the doctrine that Lucifer and our Lord, Jesus Christ, are brothers may seem surprising to some—especially to those unacquainted with latter-day revelations. But, both the scriptures and the prophets affirm that Jesus Christ and Lucifer are indeed offspring of our Heavenly Father and, therefore, spirit brothers. Jesus Christ was with the Father from the beginning. Lucifer, too, was an angel "who was in authority in the presence of God," a "son of the morning." (see the Mormon books on Doctrine and covenants 76:25-27) Both Jesus and Lucifer were strong leaders with great knowledge and influence. But as the Firstborn of the Father, Jesus was Lucifer's older brother. (See the Mormon books on Doctrine and Covenants 93:21)."

The Spiritual Law of Confession and the Spiritual Law of Dignitary Authority

out of his protective covering by ignoring God's Word. As a consequence, he gradually slipped into error.

Over the course of time, he grew doubtful of his Christian faith and was seduced into agreement with the Mormon beliefs to which he willfully exposed himself. This happened because his love for the truth was less than his lust for the woman.

Finally, the pendulum swung all the way to the dark side and he no longer could tell the difference between the truth of God and the Mormon doctrines. He ultimately denounced his Christian faith and joined the Mormon church. He called the Holy Spirit's gift as nothing more than emotionalism. Later, he told me that his Christian beliefs were total deception.

When he confessed the Mormon doctrine, he decreed a curse upon his life and was water baptized into Mormonism. To this day he remains dedicated to Mormon doctrine—a teaching created by demons. If he doesn't repent and return to Jesus Christ as defined by God's Word, he will die in unbelief and remain eternally condemned while wrapped in a disguise of religion.

And his romantic hopeful—it never happened.

★★★

Words Have Power

When Sarah heard the Lord tell Abraham that within the year she would have the promised son. She was inside the tent and laughed at the absurdity. Obviously, she stood in unbelief.

At the time, she was eighty-nine years old and Abraham was ninety-nine. The Lord confronted her and asked why she laughed, but she denied her response.

Exactly as the Lord said, a year later the promised son arrived. As a memorial to her unbelieving response, the child was given the name *Isaac,* which means "laughter".

The Spiritual Law of Confession and the Spiritual Law of Dignitary Authority

As time moved along, Isaac married a woman named Rebecca and they had twin boys. When the boys were born, Esau came first with Jacob holding the heel of his brother.

Esau grew up as a masculine man, a hunter, and Isaac favored him over Jacob.

Jacob was a tender momma's boy, and Rebecca favored him over Esau (Genesis 25:27-28).

Jacob's name means "deceiver". Throughout his life, he used cunning manipulations to get what he wanted. By deception and opportunity, he stole Esau's birthright (Genesis 27). In like manner, people treated him the same way throughout his life (Genesis 29:13-29) **(The Spiritual Law of Sowing and Reaping)**.

Through cunning deception, Jacob stayed one step ahead of those with whom he had dealings, including Laban, his father-in-law.

Not until Jacob encountered the Lord would his name be changed from "deceiver" to "Israel", meaning "prince with God".

As a father of twelve sons that became the twelve tribes of the Jewish nation, Jacob lived into the meaning of his *new* God-given name.

Again...words set the destiny of our lives.

James 3:6 speaks of the tongue as a tool of four dark potentials:

1. The tongue is a fire, the very world of iniquity.
2. The tongue is set among our members and defiles the body.
3. The tongue sets the course of our life on fire.
4. The tongue is set on fire by hell.

Quite obviously, it is not the tongue of itself that James refers to, rather, it is that part of our "unregenerated" soul through which unrighteous words are spoken.

The Spiritual Law of Confession and the Spiritual Law of Dignitary Authority

Let's Make It Personal

You have often said things that set the course and direction of your life. They were words both to the good and to evil. We all have done this.

The thoughts coming from your soul were verbalized with words that launched from your mouth. Such words were empowered by declaration.

James says:

> "For every species of birds, or reptiles, and creatures of the sea, is tamed and has been tamed by the human race, 8 but no one can tame the tongue; it is a restless evil and full of deadly poison. 9 with it we bless our Lord and Father, and with it we curse men who have been made in the likeness of God 10 from the same mouth come both blessing and cursing. My brethren these things ought not be this way." (James 3:7-10)

To avoid such damage, the Scripture says to be renewed in the "spirit of your mind".

> "Do not be conformed to this world, but be transformed by the renewing of your mind. Then you will be able to test and approve what is the good, pleasing, and perfect will of God." (Romans 12:2)

At the instant you were saved, your spirit came alive. Your soul, however, still needs complete *regeneration*. Hence, from the moment of salvation, your spirit is configured with the ability to believe God's Written Living Word, the Bible. Because you are *able* to believe, His Word continually flushes over your soul and progressively restores it.

> "...so that He might scantily her [the Christian, Christ's Bride] having cleansed her by the washing of water with the Word." (Ephesians 5:25. Square brackets by author for added clarity.)

The Spiritual Law of Confession and the Spiritual Law of Dignitary Authority

Thus, at the moment of salvation, your soul begins the "process of renewal by regeneration". To accomplish this, you must be led by God's Spirit *through* your spirit, not your soul.

Christians led by the dictates of their unregenerated soul are referred to as carnal, meaning spiritually immature.

According to the science of neurology, as you subject yourself to God's living Word, your soul is literally remapped. The old patterns of thought are changed according to the dictates of God's truth. By the Holy Spirit's superimposing power, His Word washes over your old mindsets that shaped you according to this world's ideologies, values, perspectives, and mentalities. Your soul is gradually reconfigured according to Kingdom Righteousness. It is a process, not a sudden arrival. Hebrews 4:12 explains it this way:

> *"For the Word of God is living and active and sharper than and two-edged sword and piercing as far as the division of soul and spirit, of both joints and marrow, and able to judge the thoughts and intentions of the heart."*

It's Not Metaphysical, It's Spiritual

As God's Word penetrates your soul, your conscience is reshaped according to His truths, revelations, understandings, and insights. By this, your spirit is empowered so that you are led by His Spirit rather than the lusts and desires of your unregenerated soul. However, there will always be a choice between the Holy Spirit's leading and your old familiar dark habits. Accordingly, your *will* to choose is never taken from you. It is, therefore, always a choice by what you love most: this world or the Lord.

What are you feasting on? Are you feeding your spirit with God's Word, or are you feeding your soul with the lusts of this world? If you follow the unregenerated part of your soul, you will follow the dark values of the world. Furthermore, your words will set the course of your life on fire. For this reason, keep your spirit strong by studying God's Word and stay in prayer.

The Spiritual Law of Confession and the Spiritual Law of Dignitary Authority

You are a free-will moral agent to do as you please and speak. What you confess is either licensed in the domain of God or the domain of darkness.

In the same way, if you are obedient to the Holy Spirit's leading, your spirit takes the lead and your soul follows. You are thus empowered by the Holy Spirit Words that produce life.

> *"It is the Spirit who gives life; the flesh* [that part of our unregenerated soul] *profits nothing; the Words that I have spoken to you are spirit and are life." (John 6:63. Square brackets added by author for clarity.)*

You are a free-will moral agent to do and speak as you please. You are the captain of your soul, but always accountable to God's spiritual laws. What you confess is either licensed under the domain of God or the domain of darkness.

Therefore, by understanding His spiritual laws, you will comprehend how words direct the course of life. They either release blessings or curses according to the source of their domain. After all, "words have power".

These are life and death issues. Whatever you say through agreement and alignment produces either curses or blessings. Thus, our destinies are set into motion by the very things we say.

The Spiritual Laws of Dignitary Authority and **The Spiritual Law of Confession** interplay one with the other. There is an insightful reference in Number 30:1-16 that describes the authority of these spiritual laws. I have cited the entire passage that deals with words, vows, rash statements, and how God uses the power of **Dignitary Authority**.

> *"Moses said to the heads of the tribes of Israel: "This is what the LORD commands: 2 When a man makes a vow to the LORD or takes an oath to obligate himself by a pledge* [of words uttered], *he must not break his word but must do everything he said. 3 "When*

The Spiritual Law of Confession and the Spiritual Law of Dignitary Authority

a young woman still living in her father's household makes a vow to the LORD or obligates herself by a pledge [by words uttered, literally a rash statement] 4 and her father hears about her vow or pledge but says nothing to her, then all her vows and every pledge by which she obligated herself will stand. 5 But if her father forbids her when he hears about it, none of her vows or the pledges by which she obligated herself will stand; the LORD will release her because her father has forbidden her. 6 "If she marries after she makes a vow or after her lips utter a rash promise by which she obligates herself 7 and her husband hears about it but says nothing to her, then her vows or the pledges by which she obligated herself will stand. 8 But if her husband forbids her when he hears about it, he nullifies the vow that obligates her or the rash promise by which she obligates herself, and the LORD will release her. 9 "Any vow or obligation taken by a widow or divorced woman will be binding on her. 10 "If a woman living with her husband makes a vow or obligates herself by a pledge under oath 11 and her husband hears about it but says nothing to her and does not forbid her, then all her vows or the pledges by which she obligated herself will stand. 12 But if her husband nullifies them when he hears about them, then none of the vows or pledges that came from her lips will stand. Her husband has nullified them, and the LORD will release her. 13 Her husband may confirm or nullify any vow she makes or any sworn pledge to deny herself. 14 But if her husband says nothing to her about it from day to day, then he confirms all her vows or the pledges binding on her. He confirms them by saying nothing to her when he hears about them. 15 If, however, he nullifies them some time after he hears about them, then he must bear the consequences of her wrongdoing." 16 These are the regulations the LORD gave Moses concerning relationships between a man and his wife, and between a father and his young daughter still living at home."
(Square brackets added by author for clarity.)

Because the husband has **Dignitary Authority**, he is a priest to his family—a shield and canopy over his entire household. By his God-appointed position, he has the authority to void foolish, rash statements, vows, and words. If, by passivity, indifference, or ignorance he

The Spiritual Law of Confession and the Spiritual Law of Dignitary Authority

lets certain words and decrees stand, then **The Law of Spiritual Confession** comes into play and the words are set into motion.

There is no such thing as "words that do nothing". Rather, we direct our destiny by the very things we say.

Especially by words that apply far into the future, their *"cause-and-effect"* is not easily recognized. For example, if a *young* daughter is frustrated that no man takes an interest in her and she says, "I am never going to meet anyone and get married, and I will never have children." Upon hearing this, her spiritually alert father can void her words so that her spoken curse has no power over the future of her life.

This begs the question: How many children are cursed under damaging words that their parents decreed over their children's lives when spoken in anger? How many people live by words they declared and do not understand the working of its power?

STORY: In the police department where I worked, there was a godless sergeant that was arrogantly hostile toward my Christian faith. One day he said, "If this is Christianity, I want nothing to do with it." Without realizing it, he spoke words against his life that would manifest years later.

Over the span of his career, bitterness gradually filled his soul. He carried inordinate levels of stress, was generally unhappy, and could never escape the cynical darkness that enshrouded him.

In sustained acrimony, he worked in the police department for thirty-eight years until he finally decided to retire. His house was paid off; he had a considerable retirement income; and he planned to move to Alaska where his sons lived.

The last few months before retiring, he had an unrelenting flu-like sickness. He went to the doctor and was given a thorough

The Spiritual Law of Confession and the Spiritual Law of Dignitary Authority

examination which ultimately led to exploratory surgery. When he woke up from the anesthesia, the doctor told him he had ten days to live.

A Christian pastor came to his hospital room and talked to him about salvation. Knowing that death was imminent, he gave his life to Jesus. On the tenth day after his surgery, he entered eternity in Jesus without any rewards.

Had he given his life to Jesus in his *early days*, bitterness would not have entangled in his soul and he could have lived in great peace. However, by saying that he wanted nothing to do with Jesus, his words set the course of his life. Existing without Jesus, his spoken curse opened the door to self-destruction. Through sustained stress and bitterness, cancer overwhelmed his body.

> *"A calm and peaceful and tranquil heart is life and health to the body."* (Proverbs 14:30a)

★★★

According to what we say, our tongue sets the direction of our life that leads us into either blessings or curses. This is based on **The Spiritual Law of Confession**.

Chapter Nine
The Spiritual Law of Separation and The Spiritual Law of the Canopy

"For the Lord God is a sun and shield: the Lord will give grace and glory: no good thing will He withhold from them that walk uprightly." (Psalm 84:11)

The Canopy

A canopy in both the spiritual and the natural is a covering, shelter, an umbrella, a dome of protection, and a shield. It is something set over a person's life by reason of declaration, heritage, design, purpose, or as a divine covenant. It can be practical, material, and spiritual. For example, children are under the canopy of their parents who provide shelter and material support; citizens are under the canopy of their nation by constitutional rights; police officers operate under the canopy of an empowering government that legally grants them their authority.

According to Psalms 91:1, Christians dwell under the canopy of God whose covenant provides them material, soulical, physical, and spiritual provision:

The Spiritual Law of Separation and the Spiritual Law of the Canopy

"He who dwells in the shelter of the Most High Will remain secure and rest in the shadow of the Almighty [whose power no enemy can withstand]." (*Square brackets added by author for clarity.)*

There are several examples of God's canopy shown in scripture. For instance, Lot was blessed because he lived under the canopy of Abraham's covenant with God. Whatever was joined to Abraham was blessed.

All two hundred seventy-six people on board a ship were divinely protected under Paul's canopy by God (Acts 27:1-44).

Under Jesus' canopy, none of His disciples were lost except Judas, the prophesied one, the son of perdition who betrayed Him for money. When Judas left the Lord's canopy, Satan possessed him.

The canopy, both tangible and spiritual, is a very real spiritual law of God's Kingdom.

Separation

As you advance in Christ, separation is a required principle in the process of your progress. Simply stated, at various stages of your spiritual advancement, **The Spiritual Law Of Separation** is required in order to eliminate any impeding factors related to your calling and purpose.

This includes people, activities, places—anything that hinders your forward progress in the transition of "times and seasons" throughout your life.

The Eye of the Needle

In Matthew 19:24, Jesus uses the "eye of the needle" as a metaphor to represent the process of separation.

> *"Again I say to you, it is easier for a camel to go through the eye of a needle, than for a rich man[13] to enter the kingdom of God."*

---

[13] Since this is true, what do we say of the patriarchs, such as Job, Abraham, Isaac, Jacob, David, or Solomon, or, for that matter, any wealthy person? Is it wealth Jesus

The Spiritual Law of Separation and the Spiritual Law of the Canopy

In ancient times, fortified walls surrounded the cities. At night, its massive gates were closed and barred from the inside. If a person wanted to enter the city, he had to pass through the "eye of the needle". This particular entryway was so narrow that a single camel could barely squeeze through its opening. Travelers coming inside the city first had to remove the cargo from their animal. With the animal stripped down, they led it through the narrow passage. Then, they carried their goods through the eye of the needle and again reloaded the cargo onto the animal. The process was slow and troublesome, but, it was an effective way to prevent marauding groups and armies from gaining quick access.

Along the process of our progress, we must periodically pass through the "eye of the needle". This is analogous to **The Spiritual Law of Separation** at decisive intersections of life. Anything that inhibits, hinders, impedes, or is inharmonious to purpose and advancement must be separated from us. Thus, the Lord frequently passes us through the *eye of the needle* in order to increase and expand us. It is important to recognize the moment when it is time to separate from that which does not fit our spiritual progress.

As a church moves forward, spiritual factors change and intensify. In order for it to spiritually advance, there must be unity, vision, and agreement among its leaders and congregation members at each stage of growth. Accordingly, there are various intersections where separation occurs. Issues of incompatibility naturally rise to the surface. For example, in Bill Johnson's church of Redding, California (Bethel Church), the anointing of miracles and healings suddenly manifested in the church. When the Holy Spirit's power manifested in Johnson's church, there was a dynamic shift. However, longstanding members did not like the change and they separated. They were resistant to the spiritual advancement which God assigned to Bethel Church. For those who walked away, it was a personal choice more

---

spoke about, or is it one's "dependance" upon wealth? Does wealth own the wealthy, or does the wealthy own the wealth? God desires wealth and prosperity for His people as long as they are not captive to earthly possessions.

The Spiritual Law of Separation and the Spiritual Law of the Canopy

than anything else. They rather preferred a quiet uneventful meeting without surprises or the excitement that typically come with healing and deliverance.

Jesus experienced the *separation factor* in His ministry as well. As He moved toward the completion of His purpose, He set the cost of the next phase which required covenant agreement (John 6:51-58). For that reason, many departed from Him and returned to their former associations and occupations (John 6:66. Amplified Bible). They were not willing to sacrifice what it took to be spiritually configured by God's anointing, unction, purpose, and calling at the next level with Jesus.

When God *trims* a church, people's hidden character is revealed in order to recognize the tares from the wheat (Matthew 13:24-30). Branches are trimmed from the vine (John 15:1-2); the Jezebels are identified (Revelation 2:20); and those given to divisiveness are exposed (3 John1:9). What some might term as a church split is actually a house cleaning by the Lord.

> *"They went out from us, but they were not of us; for if they had been of us, they would have remained with us; but they went out, so that it would be shown that they all are not of us."* (1 John 2:19)

> *"Can two walk together, unless they are agreed?"* (Amos 2:3)

If a congregation is resistant to what God is doing, He does one of two things: (1) He internally changes the people if they will submit to His Spirit. But if they do not want to change, then (2) He replaces them with those who embrace His purpose and direction. It is a process. This means the tares will leave; the congregation will transform; and the church will surge forward.

A stagnant church is composed of people who refuse change. They prefer to settle for substantially less than the Lord has for them. They want predictive routines. They hold ground and simply say that the old wine is good enough (Luke 5:39). However, new wine requires new wine skin and the old must leave to make room for the new thing God wants to do. When churches prefer the old over the new, sooner

The Spiritual Law of Separation and the Spiritual Law of the Canopy

or later, such churches wither and die because the pastor refuses to submit to the Holy Spirit.

Refering again to the "canopy", there are several accounts in Scripture that illustrate how **The Spiritual Law of the Canopy** operates.

Abraham

When God called Abraham, He separated him from his kinsmen and country to go to the place God would show Him (Genesis 11:31).

One reason for Abraham's separation was because his father's family were pagan idolaters. The Ur of the Chaldees was notoriously pagan and God wanted Abraham to Himself.

Abraham's destiny was to be the father of many nations. Because of that, God gave him Dignitary Authority. Through him, God raised up a Jewish nation of people, God's chosen people, a special people — the Hebrews, later to be known as the Israelites. From them came the Messiah—the Savior of the World. This plan encompassed hundreds of years to develop.

The Separation Principle

In the parable of the Wheat and Tares (Matthew 13:24-30), we find both the wheat and tares growing together. Both lived in the same soil, received the same rain, were cultivated in the same field, and seem indistinguishable one from the other...until harvest time—the time of separation.

༄༅

At various times, the Lord will pass us through the eye of the needle to prune us for advancement. He separates us from certain things, places, or people.

༄༅

At harvest time, the tares stand strong, tall, and proud. The wheat, by contrast, bows its head in humility. During harvest, the wheat is separated from the tares, and the tares are tossed into the fire.

The Spiritual Law of Separation and the Spiritual Law of the Canopy

A tare is anything that impedes or hinders your progress. At the right time, it needs to be separated from your life. Timing is everything. This includes location, people, things, activities, patterns, or habits. It is anything that interferes with forward progress.

Friends that were once compatible or even beneficial will disconnect from you simply because they don't fit the next phase of your life's purpose. They aren't necessarily enemies, but for one reason or another they don't share the same intensity, vision, commitment, or purpose. Therefore, at various times and sequences, **The Spiritual Law of Separation** naturally trims your life for advancement. Sometimes the process is painful and even confusing. But without separation, there is no advancement.

Things, people, or places that once served position and purpose suddenly become hinderances in the next phase. For example, as the Jews multiplied from seventy-five people (Acts 7:14) into a nation of three million, the land of Egypt served Israel for generations. But the time came for the Jews to separate from Egypt's covering. God wanted them in their own land as a sovereign nation. Thus He separated them from the pagan influence of the Egyptians.

The Apostle Paul

The Apostle Paul heavily persecuted the church as a zealous Jew before he converted to Jesus. He was a Pharisee and the son of a Pharisee. He was trained under leading rabbis; advancing far beyond his contemporaries in Judaism; more zealous for the law than those about him; and was highly respected in the ranks of the Sanhedrin. However, at the right time, Jesus revealed Himself to Paul and then *suddenly* everything changed.

The Spiritual Law of Separation eliminated everything that was inharmonious to Paul's purpose and calling. He lost friends, associates, privileges, gratification from his peers, and the prestige of being a Pharisee. Within the elite religious community of the Jew, he was considered an apostate and a traitor. Consequently, nobody wanted anything to do with him (Philippians 3:8).

The Spiritual Law of Separation and the Spiritual Law of the Canopy

"More than that, I count all things to be loss in view of the surpassing value of knowing Christ Jesus my Lord, for whom I have suffered the loss of all things, and count them mere rubbish, so that I may gain Christ." (Philippians 3:8)

Time and Focus

The Spiritual Law of Separation eliminates specific unrelated things that absorb time and focus. This could also include certain relationships. Are they compatible or hindering; equally yoked in vision, or slightly different?

A tare can be anything or anyone in your life that impedes or prevents your progress.

STORY: Before I was saved, I actively competed in the martial arts. A great deal of my time and focus was spent conditioning, going to various tournaments, progressing in the degree ranks of my black belt, and teaching classes at three different schools. Eventually, I won US and World titles that placed even more demand on my life.

Right after earning my 1st Degree Black Belt, I had a powerful encounter with the Lord and became an on-fire Christian. I knew I was called as a missionary to Africa. As a result, my ambitions in the martial art shifted and I was progressively drawn deeper into the Kingdom of God which captured my heart. I knew the day would come when I would have to separate from the martial art.

Parallel to my advancements in Taekwon-Do, the Lord advanced me in the knowledge and experience of His Kingdom. Finally, the time came when the Lord said, "I am calling you out of the martial art. Because of where I am taking you in your ministry, you no longer have time for it and Me both."

I quit Taekwon-Do and cut identity with it. No longer obligated to its demands, I charged forward in my calling to the nations of the world. Even though I pastored various churches, my primary call was to

The Spiritual Law of Separation and the Spiritual Law of the Canopy

teach and train leaders in countries throughout the world. They, in turn, would impart the same to the people of their culture.

Since leaving the martial art, I have traveled a distance equal to more than forty-two times around the world. Because the martial art demands incredible time and attention, it would have been impossible for me to serve the Lord and travel to the nations. Accordingly, **The Law of Separation** required me to eliminate Taekwon-Do from my life.

★★★

Recognizing the times and seasons according to your purpose and vision is vital. Moreover, you must know when close associates and friends no longer fit your vision, intensity, and purpose. This isn't to say there needs to be an unfriendly break, but when dynamics change, it needs to be recognized how they fit into your life.

> "There is an appointed time for everything. And there is a time for every event under heaven..." (Ecclesiastes 3:1)

Peter and Andrew were brothers. At the same time, they were cousins to James and John who were also brothers. All of them were in the fishing business. They owned boats and nets, had hired servants, and maintained a fairly reasonable income. But after meeting Jesus, they recognized their calling and followed Him. One season of their lives ended, and a new season began. A choice had to be made between their fishing business and following Jesus.

Paul no longer pursued his endeavors as a Pharisee. His dreams of being part of Judaism ended when he encountered Jesus. Immediately, a new season in his life started. After some fourteen years of transition, he became the foremost Foundation Apostle that reached both Jews and Gentiles even though his primary call was to the Gentiles.

After Matthew met Jesus, he no longer worked as a tax collector for the Roman government. He walked away from a lucrative position. A new season in his life started and he left everything.

The Spiritual Law of Separation and the Spiritual Law of the Canopy

The Spiritual Law of Separation always comes with a choice. Those who move forward understand the sacrifice it takes. Some people refuse the cost. Others see a greater purpose which offsets everything else and they surge forward in the Lord.

Odd as it may sound, a tare can be a brother or sister *in the Lord* who was previously harmonious and compatible during earlier seasons of your life. But as God refines and defines your calling and purpose, the road forks. They must continue where God leads them, and you must continue where God leads you. Thus, the intensity, common ground, and fellowship of former friends changes. Don't fight it. Accept it. In the next season, God assigns other people to you that are harmonious to your purpose and calling according to **The Spiritual Law of Pairing**.

If Christian friends are not called to the same walk, you cannot take them with you into the next season. This is because they do not have the same calling, vision, and purpose. As a result, they will impede your efforts. They cannot see as you see. Nor do they walk in the same grace for the work which God assigned you.

This doesn't make them an enemy or even an opposition to the Lord. Simply stated, they are not spiritually configured with the same spiritual emphasis as you are. This was the problem between Paul and John-Mark, the nephew of Barnabas. Paul's grace-gift to walk in the intensity, sacrifice, passion, drive, purpose, and focus was far more intense than what John-Mark possessed. As a consequence, very early in the missionary journey, John-Mark deserted them and turned back to Jerusalem.

෴
Separation is required from anything which impedes, hinders, or does not harmonize with God's calling, purpose, and direction upon your life. Satan uses this same law to disrupt spiritual continuity and break the power of agreement.
෴

The Spiritual Law of Separation and the Spiritual Law of the Canopy

A few years later, Paul and Barnabas decided to revisit the places they first ministered. Barnabas *again* wanted to take John-Mark, but Paul refused the plan because John-Mark lacked the endurance required of him for the challenges ahead.

Paul clearly understood that John-Mark was not called and equipped as they were. Barnabas, however, was emotionally attached to his nephew and was not factually centered. He violated **The Spiritual Law of Pairing** when he discounted God's pairing with Paul. As a result, Barnabas departed from Paul and took John-Mark—his sister's son. From that point forward, there is no record of Barnabas or his ministry in the Scriptures. Church tradition tells us that he was martyred in 61 AD at Salamis on the Island of Cyprus which was eight years before Paul was martyred.[14]

Again, separation is required from anything that impedes or hinders God's calling, purpose, and direction. Of course, this does not mean that all separations are of God. Satan uses this same law of separation to break spiritual continuity that comes through the power of divine pairing. To do this, he commonly uses the spirit of "offense".

As previously mentioned, the time came when Jesus explained the cost of following Him to the next phase of His ministry. He looked at the crowd of disciples, the Seventy (Luke 10:1); the Twelve (Luke 9:1); and others who stood with starry amazement at His power and prestige. The next phase of Jesus' ministry required that they be in covenant relationship with Him. If they were not, they could have no part of going forward under His anointing. This was a separation point that culled out those willing to pay the price from those who would not.

---

[14] According to various church records, Barnabas was martyred on Cyprus (the place of his birth) in about 61 AD by a mob stirred up by Bar-Jesus (also known as Elymas). This was the magician / false prophet that Paul's spoke a judgement against whereupon Elymas went blind for a period of time. According to ancient sources, Barnabas was preaching at a synagogue in Salamis, when a mob attacked him, dragged him out with a rope around his neck, and killed him. It is told that John Mark, who was the nephew of Barnabas, collected the body of Barnabas and buried him in this area.

The Spiritual Law of Separation and the Spiritual Law of the Canopy

Jesus and the Disciples

When Jesus spoke to those who followed Him, He spoke in covenant terms, terms that affirmed His deity as God. They clearly understood what He was saying, but many of them had no revelation that He was the Son of God. For this reason, according to the Amplified Bible, it says in John 6:66...

> *"After this, many of His disciples drew back* [returned to their old associations and occupations] *and no longer accompanied Him."*

The tares in the heart are deadly if they turn to seed. They spread and multiply. Eventually, you will know who stands with you. Time and circumstance prove all things.

The first group that departed from Jesus self-defined their position. After they left, Jesus turned to the Twelve and asked if they too wanted to leave. Peter spoke for all of them:

> *"Simon Peter answered, Lord, to whom shall we go? You have the Words (the message) of eternal life. 69 And we have learned to believe and trust, and* [moreover] *we have come to know* [with all certainty] *that You are the Holy One of God, the Christ (the Anointed One), the Son of the living God." (John 6: 68-69. The Amplified Bible. Square brackets added by author for clarity.)*

As previously stated, the separation process is painful but nonetheless required.

Storms reveal a person's friends. In the Holiday cruises of life, friendships are assumed but unproven. Until that time comes, they are little more than acquaintances.

We find an example of this referring to Judas. In John 13:1-30, Jesus washed Judas' feet. And In Psalm 41:9, again referring to Judas, it is said:

The Spiritual Law of Separation and the Spiritual Law of the Canopy

> *"Even My own close friend in whom I trusted, who ate my bread, has lifted up his heel against Me [betraying Me]."* (Square brackets added by author for clarity.)

Don't be surprised, therefore, if those who call you "friend" in the *calm* seasons of life are later on the very ones that abandon you in the storms. Do not be amazed when such things are revealed. Rather, be thankful that they are exposed for what they are.

Even Jesus experienced this reality when He called the apostles His "friends". Friends? Later on, they deserted Him and denied that they knew Him (Matthew 26:56).

> *"No longer do I call you slaves, for the slave does not know what his master is doing, but I have called you friends, for all things that I have heard from My father I have made known to you."* (John 15:15)

Classic tares are typically less than honorable people. All things are proved by time and circumstance. Eventually, you will know who stands with you.

Jesus knew what lurked in the unregenerated soul of man. For this reason, He was careful not to receive the praises of men during His earthly sojourn. Therefore, do not be surprised when *unproven* friends turn without hesitation and become your worst critics.

> *"But Jesus, for His part, did not entrust Himself to them, because He knew all people* [and understood the superficiality and fickleness of human nature], *25 and He did not need anyone to testify concerning man* [and human nature], *for He Himself knew what was in man* [in their hearts-in the very core of their being]." (John 2:24-25. Square brackets added by author for clarity.)

Gideon's Army

The story of Gideon aptly demonstrates **The Spiritual Law of Separation**. Gideon was winnowing the wheat to separate the chaff in a winepress—not the normal place for that kind of work. They were

The Spiritual Law of Separation and the Spiritual Law of the Canopy

hiding the wheat because marauding bands of Midianites frequently ravaged the Land.

Unexpectedly, the Lord appeared to Gideon and appointed him to lead Israel in a battle against their enemies. Through a series of events that proved the Lord was with him, he marshalled an army of 32,000 men. However, the Lord told him there were too many even though the ratio was 1 Israelite to every 4 Midianites. By the largeness of Gideon's numbers, if they defeated the Midianites they would claim victory as from their own strength rather than from the Lord.

God's glorification was essential for Israel's repentance and restoration. Winning the battle by their strength would further entrench their apostate condition.

God told Gideon to tell everyone who was afraid and trembling to go home. The first phase of separation revealed who was with him and who would most likely retreat in battle. As a result, 22,000 men returned to their villages. 10,000 men remained. The ratio of Israelite to Midianites change to 1 Israelite for every 13 Midianites. It now seemed unlikely that they could defeat the Midianites.

Then the Lord told Gideon to take the remaining men to the river and drink. Those who kneeled and scooped the water in their hands were to be separated from those who got down on their hands and knees and lapped the water like a dog. Again, it was self-defining.

By the same habitual posture used in Baal worship, 9,700 men lapped the water like a dog. They were brave and bold, but without affection for the Lord.

In fact, the reason why Israel was under attack was because she had departed from the Lord and worshipped idols, specifically Baal. Having left God's protective canopy, the Israelites were subject to their enemies.

Three hundred men remained. They were brave, bold, and holy. This was the army God used to defeat the Midianites. The ratio changed

The Spiritual Law of Separation and the Spiritual Law of the Canopy

again. There was only 1 Israelite for ever 450 Midianites. It was now an impossible win—except for the Lord's intervention.

By the process of elimination, God applied two laws: **The Spiritual Law of Separation** in union with **The Spiritual Law of Pairing**. By **The Spiritual Law of Pairing**, God brought everyone under the same anointing and purpose under one canopy. They stood in the union of agreement by faith in God. And, as the account unfolded, the Midianite army was defeated by Gideon as God stirred the enemy into confusion. No one of Gideon's army threw a spear, or shot an arrow.

The Canopy

The Spiritual Law of the Canopy is seen in several instances throughout Scripture where God's divine canopy is set over people's lives.

Abraham's Canopy

For the first example, we again go back to the life of Abraham. God blessed him with great wealth, but to Abraham's credit, his wealth never owned him. His abundance was so enormous that when he moved from place to place, it was like moving a tent-city.

In order to maintain his livestock, Abraham had a massive payroll of people. Added to that, he had many servants including three hundred eighteen trained men for battle. Knowing that these men were adults, it is highly probable, based on their culture, that most of them were married and had children. Reasonably, the number of people in Abraham's camp could easily have reached over one thousand people, besides the thousands of livestock. Furthermore, Abraham, as leader, was responsible for everything.

His wealth was directly related to God's covenant with him. Everyone *under* Abraham's canopy was blessed, including Lot, his nephew, a benefactor and recipient of Abraham's massive blessing.

Lot and Abraham's properties grew so enormous that eventually they required separate lands for pasturing. Accordingly, they went to a high hill that overlooked the area. Graciously, Abraham gave Lot the

The Spiritual Law of Separation and the Spiritual Law of the Canopy

first choice. Lot visually surveyed the area and selfishly chose the green and well-watered places. Abraham, however, did not look with the natural eye. He knew his prosperity came from the Lord.

Lot departed with his enormous wealth, all of which he acquired under Abraham's divine canopy. He then headed toward Sodom and Gomorrah. However, unbeknownst to Lot, leaving Abraham's canopy meant leaving the source of blessing.

Lot would eventually lose everything, including his property, servants, and even his wife. He would end up near Zoar in a cave close to a village situated by the Dead Sea. Isolated and alone, his two daughters feared they would be childless. Accordingly, they got their father intoxicated and committed incest with him. As a result, he became the patriarch of two tribes of people, the Moabites and the Ammonites, both of which became enemies of Israel.

The contrasts in Lot's life was amazing: After he departed from Abraham's canopy as a wealthy man, he eventually ended up with nothing.

Moses Canopy

Moses sent the twelve spies into the Promised Land. When they came back, ten of them gave a fearful and faithless report. They openly acknowledged that the land flowed with milk and honey, but they saw giants and were fearful.

> "There we saw the giants (the descendants of Anak came from the giants); and we were like grasshoppers in our own sight, and so we were in their sight." (Numbers 13:33)

The giants were the progeny between fallen angels and the daughters of men as reported in Genesis 6. Archeologists have discovered their remains that measured between ten and sixteen feet tall!

When the ten spies returned, they accurately recited the *facts* of their observation but they failed to balance it with *truth*. Joshua and Caleb, however, spoke the truth in faith. They saw the giants as obstacles that God would remove for them.

The Spiritual Law of Separation and the Spiritual Law of the Canopy

The ten spies, filled with fear and unbelief, communicated their concerns and transferred their fear into the people. Disheartened, the masses rose up against Moses and wanted someone to take them back to Egypt. As a result, God vowed that none of their generation over the age of twenty would enter the Promised Land, except Joshua and Caleb.

The next day, a number of Israelites regretted their decision and told Moses they decided to go into the Promised Land. However, Moses warned them about leaving their covering—God's canopy over the Israelites.

Ignoring Moses' counsel, they went into the land and quickly encountered the Amalekites and the Canaanites—the giants. Without their canopy of protection, their enemies prevailed upon them and they were struck down and beaten.

Israel's Canopy

After Moses died, God selected Joshua to lead Israel into the Promised Land. The truth is, from the time the Israelites crossed the Red Sea after leaving Egypt, it was only a ten-day march to the Promised Land. But because of the stubbornness of "that" generation, they marched in circles for forty-years until the last person died.

The day finally came when the second generation stood on the border of the Promised Land. As Israel came to the Jordan River, God wanted to prove that He was with them. He instructed the priests that carried the Ark of the Covenant to advance before the people. When the priests stepped into the river, instantly the waters upstream stopped flowing and the ground was hard and dry. The priests stood in the middle of the riverbed until all three million people with their herds and flocks crossed over.

A Chink in the Armor

Before the scepter was handed to Joshua, the tribes of Ruben, Gad, and the half-tribe of Manasseh asked Moses a question. They wanted permission to stay on the "east side" of the Jordan and set up their

The Spiritual Law of Separation and the Spiritual Law of the Canopy

occupancy apart from the other ten tribes that settled on the "west side". The east side, however, was not part of the Promised Land. Therefore, it was not under God's canopy of protection.

Their reasons for not crossing over, logical as it might seem, was because they had exceedingly larger herds and flocks than the other tribes. As such, they didn't want to share the pastureland on the west side.

Moses consented to their arrangement as long as they fought alongside the other ten tribes to conquer the Promised Land on the west side of the Jordan. They agreed to this condition, and in fact, kept their word.

However, by removing themselves from the other tribes, their detached position made them vulnerable to marauding thieves that frequently rustled their livestock and killed their herdsmen. Consequently, they did not have the peace and safety that the other tribes had under God's canopy.

Their departure from the "perfect will of God" produced curses that extended into the near and far future. Being somewhat isolated from the main body of Israelites, their vital connection was compromised. Satan seized the opportunity. As history shows, they would be the first to depart from the commandments of the Lord and commit idolatry. They were also be the first to be taken captive by another nation, specifically, Assyria (1 Chronicles 5:25-26).

Centuries later, their land was known as the Gadarenes—the place where Jesus encountered the fierce demon-possessed man. The occupants of this land raised thousands of pigs—an expressly unclean animal that the Jews were not allowed to physically touch.

I have seen the same dynamics connected with many Christians. Their relationship to the local church is weak, inconsistent, and mostly aloof. They come and go at will and have extended blocks of time away from the saints. In principle, they camp on the wrong side of the Jordan. They are non-invested, independent, place little or no value on fellowship, and are perfect targets of the enemy. Typically,

The Spiritual Law of Separation and the Spiritual Law of the Canopy

such Christians are laden with troublesome cyclical issues. The enemy attacks their children, health, and spiritual vitality. But as long as their names are written in the Lamb's Book of Life, as they reason, nothing else matters. Sadly, their lives are filled with defeat and surround-around problems.

Paul's Canopy

When Paul was on a prisoner ship traveling to Rome, they encountered a violent storm called a "Euroquilo". For many days there was no sun and no one ate any food. Growing more concerned about their survival, the ship's crew threw the tackle overboard to lighten the load.

Everyone was in peril for their life. However, an angel appeared to Paul and said, "Do not be afraid, Paul. You must stand before Caesar, and behold, God has granted you the lives of all those sailing with you" (Acts 27:6-44).

The canopy was set, not only for Paul, but for all two hundred seventy-six people onboard. As long as they stayed under Paul's canopy, their lives would be spared.

As the storm continued, a few sailors feared the ship would crash on the rocks and break apart. Secretly, they tried escaping in a small lifeboat.

However, Paul went to the Centurion, the man in charge of the crew. He warned him, saying, "Unless these men remain in the ship, you yourselves cannot be saved."

The Centurion believed his word, cut the ropes attached to the lifeboat, and let it float away. As it turned out, even though the ship broke apart on the rocks near the island of Malta, *everyone* made it safely to shore.

When people reject authority and separate themselves without an appointed covering, they are vulnerable to the enemy's ploys.

The Spiritual Law of Separation and the Spiritual Law of the Canopy

The Canopy and Authority

When *righteous authority* occupies its position, the Spiritual canopy of protection remains in place. But when people reject righteous authority and separate themselves without a God-appointed covering, they are immediately vulnerable to the enemy. This is the common plight of roaming, freelance, and self-willed Christians that function without a canopy. They decide their own plan apart for any consideration of the Lord. Most of all, they are NOT led by the Holy Spirit.

At one point in Paul's ministry, he was in Miletus and sent for the elders in Ephesus to bid them farewell. He knew they would never see him again. This means, of course, that Paul's apostolic authority would be removed over their lives and their canopy would change. In consideration of that, he gave a sobering prophetic warning:

> *"And now, behold, I know that all of you, among whom I went about preaching the kingdom, will no longer see my face. 26 Therefore, I testify to you this day that I am innocent of the blood of all men. 27 For I did not shrink from declaring to you the whole purpose of God. 28 Be on guard for yourselves and for all the flock, among which the Holy Spirit has made you overseers, to shepherd the church of God which He purchased with His own blood. 29 I know that after my departure savage wolves will come in among you, not sparing the flock; 30 and from among your own selves men will arise, speaking perverse things, to draw away the disciples after them. 31 Therefore be on the alert, remembering that night and day for a period of three years I did not cease to admonish each one with tears."* (Acts 20:25-31)

With Paul's canopy removed, Satan seized the opportunity to sweep in and occupy the vacant seat. By using the hidden character flaws of other "Christians", Satan would do exactly as Paul warned them. But as long as Paul was in position, the secret ambitions that lurked in the hearts of different malcontents was restrained and held in check.

The Spiritual Law of Separation and the Spiritual Law of the Canopy

The Prodigal Son

Luke Chapter 15 tells the story of the prodigal son—a young man who demanded his inheritance before it was due. In the culture of the biblical era, the inheritance was considered rightful property. If the son demanded it earlier than scheduled, he could take his father to court, however, he would have to pay a penalty for what essentially was an "early withdrawal".

In this case, the father graciously gave it to his son. Soon thereafter, the son gathered his inheritance consisting of flocks, money, servants, and clothes. He then set out on a long journey to a distant city to discover the pleasures of life.

In the distant city, his reputation as a reveler spread throughout the region. He squandered his inheritance on prostitutes, alcohol, gambling, and various pleasures until all that he had was gone. Destitute and nearly starving, he ended up tending pigs and was so hungry at times that he was willing to eat their food.

When he came to his senses, he thought about his father's servants and how they lived a better life than he had. Accordingly, he got up and returned home.

Along the way, he prepared what he would say to his father. He felt he was no longer worthy of being his son. He would ask the father to receive him as one of the hired servants.

His words were based on the assumption that he lost his "sonship" and that he was no better than a slave.

By the time he reached home, he was malnourished, dressed in rags, soiled, filthy, in poor health, smelling like pigs, destitute, barefooted, and hungry.

He had prepared his speech which he would humbly recite to his father. He canceled all hope of every regaining what he lost and resolved to live the life of an indentured servant.

The Spiritual Law of Separation and the Spiritual Law of the Canopy

The point where you leave is the place where you reenter. According to the law of continuity, there are no skipping steps in the progress of spiritual advancement.

As the son approached his father's home, His father saw him from a great distance away and ran to meet him. He grabbed his son and kept hugging him.

Standing in the presence of his father and the servants, the son courageously said, "Father, I have sinned against Heaven and against you, and I am no longer worthy to be your son."

The father ignored his son's words. Instead, he ordered the special festive coat to be brought from the house and put on his son. Then he put a ring on his son's finger, shoes on his feet, and ordered the special reserved fatted calf to be prepared for a celebration meal.

What really happened in this story? There are five considerations and five steps to his son's restoration.

In the first consideration, *the son's first step* was humbly confessing his sin and asking forgiveness of his father. He left his father's canopy as a self-confidence, arrogant, and prideful young man. This was the place where he left and it was the same place where he had to reenter.

When he left his father's canopy, it was premature and ahead of the *due time* within the proper sequence of righteous progression. The enemy, realizing the son had no protection, strategically devoured everything he had. The son could have received his inheritance and remained with his father until the proper time, but leaving the father's canopy ahead of the sequence of righteous progression proved disastrous.

In the second consideration, when he returned to his father, he returned to his father's canopy. This is the point of reentry. The *special*

The Spiritual Law of Separation and the Spiritual Law of the Canopy

coat which the father put over his son's rags symbolized the *coat of righteousness*. **This was the son's *second step*** –his restoration, the restoration of his righteousness. This particular coat was reserved for special occasions. It was made of many colors and designated for the head of the house.

In the third consideration, the father put a ring on his son's finger. **This was the third step**—the son's restoration of authority. The ring signified authority—not the son's authority, but the authority of his father that the son could again represent. It was a signet ring used for pressing into soft wax when something was sealed.

In the fourth consideration, the father put shoes on his son's feet. **This was the fourth step**—the son's restoration to freedom. Slaves did not wear shoes until their freedom was restored. The son was no longer a slave to sin.

In the fifth consideration, the fatted calf was a *covenant meal*. **This was the fifth step**—the restoration of covenant relationship with his father.

The moment he left his father's canopy, the *sword* commenced until all that he had was devoured, including his righteous standing, authority, freedom, and relationship with his father. When he returned to his father's canopy, he regained his *position in the sequence of righteous progression* which again started his prosperity.

Despite the son's reentry, the government of his sin remained. However, his reputation as a reveler would be remembered forever. The only offset would be the evidence of a proven new life. It would take time and process to regain his losses.

In most cases, the canopy can be restored but only by the Lord. Repentance through humility is the first step. There are no short cuts and no skipping spaces. Where you leave off is where you restart. The same is true regarding spiritual advancement. There is no shortcut in the sequence of righteous progression.

The Spiritual Law of Separation and the Spiritual Law of the Canopy

I have watched remorseful Christians try to circumvent **The Spiritual Law of Continuity** after regretting their actions. They leave their God-assigned canopy through offense, self-serving interests, or disregard for spiritual authority. They presumptuously reassign themselves to something else, or somewhere else, or place themselves under someone more appealing. They do not move forward, but laterally shift from one thing to another. In fact, in most cases, they fall backward. They self-assign their spiritual position and weary themselves with efforts ending in futility. Without God's wisdom, they design their own future and then wonder why their lives remain in scramble.

There is Something in a Name

When a man and woman marry, the woman's canopy over her life changes. She is no longer under her father's canopy.

She takes the name of her husband and places herself under his canopy. This is God's design, not man's design. We see this same covenant-canopy where Abram and Sarai enter in covenant with God.

The Hebrew name for God is YHWH—a sacred, unpronounceable name. When the Lord set His covenant-canopy over Abram and Sarai, He changed their names. He took the letters "H" of His name and added them to their names. Abram became AbraHam. And Sarai became SaraH.

If a wife refuses her husband's name, she compromises the canopy of her covenant. Again, "words have power". This principle is evident throughout the Scriptures. Seldom, however, is this part of the covenant noticed in the working of God's spiritual laws.

The name is the covenant, and the covenant is the canopy. Identification with the name is identification with the canopy. When a wife hyphenates her name, she is less than fully identified with the canopy of her husband. It is the same if she refuses her husband's name altogether. This is **The Spiritual Law of Identification**.

Until we identify with that to which we are bonded, the covenant is inherently weak. Accordingly, it is a conflicted canopy. In such cases,

The Spiritual Law of Separation and the Spiritual Law of the Canopy

the solidarity of covenant is fractured in such things as harmony, finances, properties, agreements, spiritual unity, integration, etc.

Mobile Independent Christians

God's Kingdom is not a shopping venture where people go from place to place looking for the best deal. The Spirit of God assigns people to a church and its leaders. Many Christians fail to realize this, especially those who are immature and unsubmitted to the Lordship of Jesus.

Independent solo walking Christians are obligated to nothing but themselves. Typically, they are infants in Christ—self-centered, carnal, immature, and ignorant of God's spiritual laws.

They move from church to church, sit under one leader, get offended, change leaders, sit under someone else for a while, and then for any reason, run to another church. They never form roots and have no commitment. The never develop endurance and never learn to manage relationships. They are self-serving and unfaithful except to themselves. The cycle goes on and on. They never mature in faith; they never obligate to anything. Yet, they claim deep spiritual insight, most of which is empty chatter.

> **Independent Christians are their own enemy. Satan has them precisely where he wants them: useless in the Body of Christ, without spiritual credibility and committed to nothing but themselves.**

It is not Satan who is their enemy—he needs do nothing. They are their own enemy. Satan has them precisely where he wants them: useless to the Body of Christ, without spiritual credibility, committed to nothing; blind to their spiritual ineptness; having no virtue of faithfulness and endurance; constantly on the move; and never releasing the potential God has for them. They are like potted plants which are uprooted and replanted every ten days. They function without

The Spiritual Law of Separation and the Spiritual Law of the Canopy

accountability; submit to no spiritual authority above themselves; are unmoved, aloof, and indifferent to the Holy Spirit's work in the *local church*. Consequently, throughout the time and seasons of their life, they miss major impartations of the Lord.

Until they humble themselves, submit to God's Spiritual Laws of faithfulness, humility, endurance, steadfastness, honor, and Kingdom Authority, they will never rise above their cyclic patterns.

They violate God's **Spiritual Law of the Canopy** in addition to a plethora of other spiritual laws. They wonder why they cannot spiritually progress in the Body of Christ. For them, the weakness of their inconsistency is their normal approach to the Kingdom. They estimate their usefulness based on what they find pleasing according to whatever gifts they possess. However, God's focus is upon the "fruit of the Holy Spirit"—the manifestation of true character forged in the fires of time-tested faithfulness and reliability. Sadly, flittering Christians have no "Body of Christ" endorsement.

They live under the cloud of insufficient finances, are routinely passed over in promotions, and have ongoing cyclic issues without resolve. They are unstable and little more than free-floating radicals in the Body of Christ. Without submitting to the Lord's assigned canopy, they cannot be nurtured and have no credible standing among the Saints. Sadly, the Lord cannot entrust them with an effective persuasive anointing.

"Independent Christians" have little or no understanding of the Canopy. Nor do they understand Kingdom Authority. They are spiritually retarded. They have no concept of those whom the Lord sets over their lives. They deem His leaders as equal to themselves and devalue Dignitary Authority that God uses for their spiritual advancement. By demeaning and rejecting those whom the Lord sets over their lives—those whom the Lord anoints, equips, and sets into position of authority, they can NEVER be promoted in the Kingdom. This is because He cannot trust spiritual authority to those who do not recognize it in others.

The Spiritual Law of Separation and the Spiritual Law of the Canopy

Solo and aloof Christians do not understand the value of commitment to the local body. They come and go whenever they want without any concern for the other members of the church. They are politely selfish and give no thought to Kingdom structure. They are self-serving, independent, and cordially unsubmitted. Their silent motto is, "Who made you the boss of me?"

Having allegiance to no one except themselves, they are inflated by their own confidence. Yet, they struggle with any truth that corrects them. They speak in spiritual terms with their Christian brethren while personally avoiding spiritual authority and Kingdom Design.

> *"These people draw near to Me with their mouth, and honor Me with their lips, but their heart is far from Me.'"* (Matthew 15:8)

They move from place to place with the agenda of *using, consuming, and moving on*. They are "time-takers" and "soul-suckers". They drain those around them, but give little or nothing in return. They rarely contribute to the local body. In their own minds, they are self-elevated by their subjective experiences and tout themselves as being spiritually astute. The Scripture describes them in the book of Jude:

> *"But these people revile the things which they do not understand... 12 they are hidden reefs in your love feasts when they feast with you without fear, caring only for themselves, clouds without water, carried along by winds, autumn trees without fruit, 13 wild waves of the sea, casting up their own shame like foam, wandering stars, for whom the black darkness has been reserved forever 16 they are grumblers, fault finders, following after their own lusts. They speak arrogantly, flattering people for the sake of gaining advantage... 19 These are the ones who cause division, are worldly minded, devoid of the Spirit. 20 But you beloved, building yourselves up on your most holy faith, praying in the Holy Spirit, 21 keep yourselves in the love of God, waiting anxiously for the mercy of our Lord Jesus Christ to eternal life."* (Jude 1:10-16, 19-21)

> *"Let no one defraud you of your prize by insisting on mock humility and the worship of angels, [or] going into detail about

The Spiritual Law of Separation and the Spiritual Law of the Canopy

visions [he claims] he has seen [to justify his authority], puffed up [in conceit] by his unspiritual mind, 19 and not holding fast to the head [of the body, Jesus Christ [which is to devalue the principles of Kingdom Design], from whom the entire body, supplied and knit together by its joints and ligaments, grows with the growth [that can come only] from God." (Colossians 2:18-19. Square brackets by author for added clarity.)

The Platform of Advancement

Every Christian advances on three platforms: (1) Humility. (2) Knowing the truth according to God's Word and (3) Submission to God's Kingdom Authority.

Jesus paid for our sin, took out the dividing wall, and gave us glorious entry into His Unshakable Kingdom. But, to the surprise of many, our great and merciful Lord Jesus did not deliver anyone from the spiritual laws that govern His Kingdom. These are the laws by which His Kingdom is established and function in all its precepts. Being designed in righteousness and justice, God's spiritual laws are designed to bring blessing to those that are humble enough to discover their treasure and obey them. But, they also bring a sword against the proud.

> *"Keep back your servant from presumptuous sins; let them not have dominion over me: then shall I be upright, and I shall be innocent from the great transgression."* (Psalm 19:13)

STORY: A dear family in my church was commissioned to write a book researching log homes. This project required extensive travel throughout America. Consequently, it took them from their church for months at a time.

They loved the Lord and were good-hearted people. But, they were seriously entangled by the project which had a timeline for completion. Even though the project was noble, I was reminded of wise counsel that Mario Murillo once said to me: "Don't get good at something good that you're not supposed to be doing."

The Spiritual Law of Separation and the Spiritual Law of the Canopy

I spoke with them about their diminishing spiritual strength. I exhorted them to reestablish closer fellowship with the church, and especially in the study of God's Word and in prayer. They graciously acknowledged my counsel, but, knowing the demand required of them to complete their book, I doubted they would follow the advice. After all, what was the urgency? They loved the Lord. He loved them. They were both going to Heaven, and there were no ripples in their pond.

When the book was finally published, they wrote a dedication to me on the inside page. Then came reviews and signings in different locations. The book was popular in its genre and did well in the market. Of no surprise, they were commissioned to write another book by the same publisher.

My heart sunk.

The same demand of time came with the second book. I could see their spiritual inventory fading by degrees. I again met with them to warn them. I shared a proverb the Lord gave me: "In the day of peace, sow your seed; and in the day of crisis, reap your harvest."

I explained that in a fallen world, we are subject to many trials and tribulations that suddenly befall us (Acts 14:22). I emphasized that we must stay vitally connected to the Lord and the local body of Believers that He uses to minister one to the other.

I further explained that in the Spirit we must be ready, proactive, and spiritual armed when trials and tribulations come. A "reactive" position is a defensive position where it is impossible to defeat your opponent.

Then it happened.

While on the road, the wife became sick. As soon as they returned home, she went to the doctor and discovered she had fast-acting liver cancer. The doctor told her she needed to stop and rest.

The Spiritual Law of Separation and the Spiritual Law of the Canopy

I could see her fear and regret. She was spiritually starved and caught off-guard.

She poured herself into regaining lost spiritual ground. Her words and recitations of Scripture were all the correct answers, but they lacked revelation and power. They were words of hope that never transitioned into faith. Even though she tried to be positive about things, and even though she returned to the fellowship of the Holy Spirit and connected again with her church, before she could regain her spiritual strength, she died.

★★★

Was her absence from church the problem? Of itself, no. Was it her work that left little or no time for Kingdom matters? Of itself, no. Was it her diminished prayer time and lack of daily nurturing in the Scriptures? Of itself, no.

Independent Christians are the most difficult people to stabilize. They are the lone sheep that habitually wander, but keep within eye-sight of the flock.

Satan is the great *one percenter*. He patiently moves one percent at a time; a little here; a little there; a constant drip; and slow but steady drain.

Her problem was the combination of all things. She was running on empty. For months at a time, she and her husband removed themselves from their canopy. They were disconnected from any fellowship with the Saints and the Lord. They rarely drew from the reservoir of the Holy Spirit. They assumed their salvation was intact—and it was. Unfortunately, they improperly estimated their spiritual vulnerability. They were weak and susceptible to the ploys of the enemy. Their independent philosophy as Christians rationalized many core essential requirements. Satan attacked by chipping away 1% at a time. He worked imperceptible specific strategies in order to gain advantage.

The Spiritual Law of Separation and the Spiritual Law of the Canopy

During their prolonged absence, we had powerful moves of the Holy Spirit in church, including healings, breakthroughs in the power of God's presence, incredible visitations, and many spiritual promotions and impartations. Sadly, they were not part of anything. They missed every impartation of the Lord's refreshing times.

If their natural eyes could have seen their spiritually emaciated condition, it would have alarmed them. They would have quickly done anything needed to regain their health. But in the unseen spiritual dimension, they had no concept of their weakness. This is exactly what Satan looks for as he stalks about like a wolf hunting for the vulnerable and presumptuous sheep.

Independent Christians are perhaps the most difficult people to stabilize in the Spirit. All looks well on the outside with smiles and happy hugs when they come to church. But, in truth, they are enamored with their own philosophy, politely stubborn, limitedly teachable, cordially resistant to authority, and extremely vulnerable to the enemy's attacks.

They are the lone sheep that continually wander at the fringes yet stay within eyesight of the flock. By presumption they are indifferent to the wolves that patrol the outer edges of the flock.

When troubles strike their families, they are spiritually disconnected and surprised by Satan's schemes. Sometimes they come back to church seeking an instant remedy. Inwardly, however, they have no intentions to change anything regarding their approach to the Kingdom. When they call on God's promises, it is largely superficial. They know what to *say*, but there is no strength within them. Being ignorant of God's spiritual laws, they foolishly maintain their present course of destruction until they are consumed by the Devourer.

It reminds me of a British warship that saw a light in the dark of the night while sailing the ocean. He signaled and said, "Suggest you change course. We are in a direct line of collision."

The return signal answered: "Suggest YOU immediately change YOUR course."

The Spiritual Law of Separation and the Spiritual Law of the Canopy

The captain of the warship confidently replied, "We are a British warship. Change your course at once."

The return signal said: "I am a lighthouse on the rocks".

Sooner or later, independent Christians end up on the rocks because they cannot read the signals.

Chapter Ten
The Spiritual Law of Pairing

"Furthermore, you shall not intermarry with them; you shall not give your daughters to their sons, nor shall you take their daughters for your sons. 4 "For they will turn your sons away from following Me to serve other gods; then the anger of the LORD will be kindled against you and He will quickly destroy you."
(Deuteronomy 7:3-4)

Three spiritual laws, **The Spiritual Law of Pairing**; **The Spiritual Law of Agreement**; and **The Spiritual Law of Continuity** work in concert.

When there is righteous pairing, there is agreement and continuity. But when **The Spiritual Law of Pairing** is violated, agreement and continuity is broken.

God divinely arranges pairing for our betterment, advancement, and promotion. Yet, when we defiantly or unwittingly enter into agreement by mispairing, especially when it seems right and spiritual, it is hindering, and in some cases, disastrous.

When **The Spiritual Law of Pairing** is righteously applied, power is released through the combined strengths of agreement. When the same spiritual law is wrongly applied, it is a source of disruption, frustration, and confusion.

According to this principle, God gives the following edicts:

The Spiritual Law of Pairing

"Do not plant your vineyard with two types of seed; if you do, the entire harvest will be compromised, both the crop you plant and the fruit of your vineyard. 10 Do not plow with an ox and a donkey yoked together. 11 Do not wear clothes of wool and linen together." (Deuteronomy 22:9-10)

"No one puts a patch of unshrunk cloth on an old garment, for the patch pulls away from the garment and worse tear result." (Matthew 9:16)

"Nor do people put new wine into old wineskins, otherwise the wineskins bursts, and the wine pours out and the wineskins are ruined, but they put new wine in fresh wineskins and both are preserved." (Matthew 9:17)

"So because you are lukewarm [spiritually useless], *and neither hot nor cold, I will vomit you out of My mouth* [rejecting you with disgust]*." (Revelation 3:16. Square brackets added by author for clarity.")*

The Spiritual Parallels of Wrong Paring

Two Types of Seed
Ox and Donkey
Wool and Linen
New and Old Wineskins
New Patch Old Material
Neither Hot Nor Cold

While these are literal tangible examples of wrong pairing, they also convey spiritual parallels as well. Fundamentally, their mispairing makes them weak and compromised.

Two Types of Seed—Deuteronomy 22: 9

"When I say to the righteous that he shall surely live, but he trusts in his own righteousness and commits iniquity, none of his righteous works shall be remembered; but because of the iniquity that he has committed, he shall die." (Ezekiel 33:13)

The Spiritual Law of Pairing

Ezekiel speaks of two mixed seeds: God's righteousness and man's self-righteousness—man trusting in his own wisdom and the credit of his works versus God's righteousness imputed through Jesus Christ. Two different platforms; both different one from the other. Both are spiritual, and both seem initially correct.

God's **Spiritual Law of Pairing** prohibits us from *trusting* in our works and self-righteousness. This is because man's works are filthy rags before the Lord (Isaiah 64:6). Therefore, if we add good works for personal endorsements to the pure sacrifice of Jesus, it is mispaired with God's righteousness and it pollutes the integrity of Jesus' offering. It is mixed seed!

Naturally, good works come as a result of the Lord's influence upon our lives. But at no time does God use our works as endorsements for being righteous. Righteousness comes exclusively through Jesus Christ's finished work.

In the spiritual application, mismatched pairing creates compromise. The components work as liabilities one against the other.

To emphasize the point: whenever a person endorses himself by good works in combination with Christ's righteousness, it is rejected by God. Apart from Jesus' sacrifice, our Heavenly Father completely rejects good works in His presence as a justification. ONLY the blood of Jesus imputes righteousness to us. Anything added to or taken from His pure sacrifice pollutes the offering of His blood. Again, it is mixed seed and dangerously misleading. In truth, this is the bedrock of legalism: works added to the cross of Jesus.

The Jewish leaders arrogantly justified crucifying God's Son, Jesus Christ, for not following their standard of righteousness. Even though they had vast knowledge of the Scriptures, they were *self-righteous* and blind. As such, they missed the truth altogether.

Ox and Donkey—Deuteronomy 22:10

"You shall not plow with an ox and a donkey together."

The Spiritual Law of Pairing

The Spiritual Law of Pairing requires *equal yoking*. This immutable law produces great blessing when obeyed, or great disaster when violated.

When a married couple is equally yoked, three dynamics form the powerbase of their agreement: unity, intensity, and vision.

Consider the problems of a mispaired married couple: They are both Christians which gives them unity in salvation. What if one spouse is called into the ministry, and the other wants nothing to do with it? They are both saved, but they have different visions.

> Where strength and endurance is required,
> never take a spiritually weak person into battle.
> They will compromise and exasperate the strong.

What happens when members of a leadership team have different visions, intensities, methods, and views of Scripture? Their corporate strength is only as strong as the level of their common agreement. Consequently, strife and confusion enter because of mispairing.

EXAMPLE: Marriage is a covenant where the husband and wife share assets and liabilities. But what happens when the wife refuses to accept the husband's last name, keeps her finances separate from his, and holds her properties as "hers" and not "theirs"? The marriage covenant is fractured with intrinsic weakness which compromises the strength of agreement. In such cases, the husband's relationship with his wife is fractured because their agreement is conditionally limited. Eventually, weakness manifests at an opportune time and produces insecurity. The fracture lines of agreement soon widen. Doubt enters. Disagreements increase and strife gains a functional position. The marriage eventually polarizes and its strength reduces to the lowest level of common agreement.

Wool and Linen—Deuteronomy 22:11

"You shall not wear a garment of different sorts, such as wool and linen mixed together."

The Spiritual Law of Pairing

In combination, these fabrics compromise each other. Linen is a stronger standalone fabric than wool. Wool, on the other hand, is a warmer fabric than linen.

When combined, wool weakens linen, and linen makes wool less heat retentive.

In the union of two things where one factor impedes the other, mispairing limits the potential. This is true in both the spiritual and the natural. When strength is paired with weakness, strength is compromised. Never laminate weak character with strong character; nor greed with generosity; nor faithfulness with infidelity. Weakness is the governing factor that reduces corporate strength.

Where endurance is required, never align spiritually weak people with strong people. Weak charactered people are predisposed to surrender. They will compromise the effort for victory.

Paul and Barnabas were divinely paired by God (Acts 13: 2). On their first missionary journey, Barnabas wanted John-Mark to accompany them. However, because John-Mark did not possess the spiritual fortitude of endurance, he deserted them and returned home. He was mispaired. This ultimately split the relationship between Paul and Barnabas—a relationship which God had divinely ordained.

New and Old Wineskins—Matthew 9:17

> "And no one puts new wine into old wineskins; otherwise the wine will burst the skins, and the wine is lost and the skins as well; but one puts new wine into fresh wineskins."

Within a week after new grape juice is poured into a wineskin, it starts fermenting and gradually stretches the skin.

Since an old skin is stretched to its maximum size, it cannot be used with new wine. The new wine overstretches an old skin and the skin bursts.

Character and the Anointing

Great character is required to contain great anointing. Therefore, before the Lord increases one's anointing, He first creates the wineskin

The Spiritual Law of Pairing

for *new-wine*. Without the proper wineskin, the end is worse than the beginning. For this reason, God first forms character to prevent failure. At the forefront of spiritual success and blessing, God-like character is always required.

Based on **The Spiritual Law of Pairing**, Jesus always enlarges character before He adds greater anointing. The two factors, character and anointing, must be compatible one to the other.

Humility forms character in order to contain power. Those wanting more from the Lord must go through His refining fires. The stretching is painful. Only champions that are trained in endurance will pay the price of suffering for the prize of victory.

When young Shirley Strand, a highly accurate prophetess, saw how God used Kathryn Kuhlman in signs, wonders, miracles, and salvation, she asked what the anointing cost her. Kathryn leaned into Shirley's face and with very slow foreboding word said, "Ev-er-y-thing."

A great majority of lottery winners end with personal failure and bitter regret. But why? How could such an enormous blessing bring disappointment? The answer is simple: They *suddenly* possessed the power and privilege that money buys. However, they did not have the character and wisdom to manage it. Every flaw in their life was amplified and it became the Parodical Son's story.

When pairing works through righteous arrangement and Kingdom Authority, it produces exponential power. The same principle is true when mispairing occurs: the outcome is exponentially disastrous.

New Patch Old Material—Matthew 9:16

"No one puts a patch of unshrunk cloth on an old garment, for the patch pulls away from the garment and a worse tear results."

When unshrunk cloth is sewn onto shrunken material, the new patch eventually shrinks and tears away. This makes the hole even worse. Common sense, right? Yet people frequently violate **The Spiritual Law of Pairing** in various ways. They combine foolishness with wisdom, and weakness with strength.

The Spiritual Law of Pairing

Ability, responsibility, and accountability should always be equal. When one's responsibility is greater than one's ability, it creates problems. Never mispair responsibility with inability. Nor make one's accountably greater than their responsibility. For example, a law enforcement officer's authority is limited to the area of his jurisdiction. His accountability is limited to the domain of his responsibility. He is not accountable beyond the borders of his responsibility as defined by his jurisdiction.

> **Never place unproven people at the helm of responsibility. Invariably, it causes problems and impedes the process of progress.**

As in the natural domain, so it is in the spiritual domain. With power comes responsibility. With anointing, comes ability. God never mispairs power, anointing, and character. He always emphasizes character before anointing because anointing produces power, and power in the hands of people without character ends in ruin.

It is a high-risk pairing to place people of *unproven character* at the helm of responsibility even if their ability meets or exceeds the position's requirement. Not knowing a person's character could potentially end in disaster. The risk is never worth the loss.

In all aspects of pairing, character is the first consideration.

Mario Murillo, a wonderful friend, has astounding salvations, healings, and miracles in his ministry. Christians swarm to be a part of his ministry. What they see is the *end product* of a man shaped by God. What they don't see is the price he paid for the Lord to navigate him into spiritual position where character and the Spirit's anointing are unified in strength.

Untested, unproven, and naive Christians do not understand the sacrifice it takes to preach the Gospel. They blissfully dive in and soon discover that a violent war exists in the unseen realm. They are shocked because they have *never* passed through the fires of refinement. They are out of context in their setting. They are unshrunk cloth that still needs to be prepared.

The Spiritual Law of Pairing

> *Time and circumstance prove all things. You never know who your friends are on the Holiday cruises of life. It takes a storm to reveal them.*

The Apostle John addressed this syndrome in 1 John 2:19 where he describes the mispairing of unshrunk cloth sewn to field tested material:

> *"They went out from us, but they were not really of us; for if they had been of us, they would have remained with us; but they went out that it might be shown they all are not of us."*

As Mario once told me, "Never trust a man that walks without a limp." He is unproven, unrefined, and without affirmation of commitment.

Just Wait and See

Time and circumstance prove all things. On the holiday cruises of life, one never knows who his true friends are. Friends are proven in the storms as those that stay with you. Unfaithful and shallow acquaintances are always the first to abandon ship. In cowardly retreat, they flee while thinking only of themselves. These are the very people that perch like vultures and while looking for opportunity at the cost of others.

> *"There are "friends" that pretend to be friends, but there is a friend that sticks closer than a brother."* (Proverbs 18:24. Quotation marks by author for added emphasis.)

The Gospel is set in the context of war. It requires soldiers of the cross, people who are unafraid to battle and press forward against adverse conditions. Battles prove the caliber of a soldier—not the bootcamp. In bootcamp, everything is theoretical. War is reality.

Jesus did not pursue the rich young ruler who walked away after He told him the answer that he sought (Matthew 19:16).

The Spiritual Law of Pairing

Jesus did not pursue the disciples that left Him when He outlined the cost. They returned to their old associations and occupations (John 6:66).

Jesus did not pursue Judas who traded Him for money (John 13:27).

Paul did not pursue Demas who left him and returned to the world. (2 Timothy 4:10).

Their final act defined their character—the real person.

Those who are categorical unshrunk cloth look for something that requires nothing of them. They want victory without sacrifice. They want glory without giving anything. They are mispaired with those willing to sacrifice everything.

Never rescue a *quitter*. Do not pursue them. If you do, nothing in their character is changed. In the end, all you have is a coward in the battle. Let them walk away! Until they inwardly change, they are mispaired and out of context with those fighting for victory.

> *"And yet they have no firm root in themselves, but are only temporary; then, when affliction or persecution occurs because of the word, immediately they fall away." (Mark 4:17)*

Talent and skill are never substitutes for character. Too often we emphasize talent and skill as a greater value than character which is forged in the fire through time and circumstance. Musicians, for example, are a dime a dozen. But a person whose talent and skill is combined with Spirit-formed character is a rare combination. They are faithful, enduring, visionary, and tenacious.

Neither Hot Nor Cold—Revelation 3:15-16

> *"I know your deed, that you are neither hot nor cold, I wish you were hot or cold. 16 So because you are lukewarm and neither hot or cold, I will spit you out of My mouth."*

When hot and cold is paired, it produces a lukewarm temperature. Lukewarm character is uncommitted and indifferent. Champions disdain this in others.

The Spiritual Law of Pairing

Jesus is a champion warrior. It disgusts Him when people surrender in battle and turn back. Tepid Christians are those who laugh, smile, frolic, and dance in the calm of life. But when it comes to the battleline that demands enduring hardship, they are the first to surrender.

> **A lukewarm Christian is a pairing of both hot and cold. Jesus, as a warrior, is disgusted by those who commit to nothing.**

Paul prophesied about weak charactered Christians in the *great falling away* before the return of the Lord (2 Thessalonians 2:3). It is interesting that the verb tense used to describe *falling away* means by graduated degrees, slowly, by increments; not suddenly.

Unless they repent, tepid Christians will never be champions of faith. They live compromised lives serving their own interests and consistently follow the path of least resistance. They place no value on eternal truths but at easily persuaded by temporal gains. Their Kingdom approach is froth with excuses. They are self-deceived and foolishly estimate their strength.

> *Now these things [their failures ending in judgment] happened to them as an example and warning [to us]; they were written for our instruction [to admonish and equip us], upon whom the ends of the ages have come. 12 Therefore let the one who thinks he stands firm [immune to temptation, being overconfident and self-righteous], take care that he does not fall [into sin and condemnation].* (1 Corinthians 10:11-12. Square brackets added by author for clarity.)

Despite their flowery words and saccharine accolades about loving Jesus, you will not find them in the ranks of proven champions.

Loyalty, faithfulness, endurance, emphasis on Kingdom values, and finishing the course as long distance runners—these are the essential virtues God looks for.

Tepid Christians are short distance sprinters. They start with great drive but quickly drop out. In their lukewarm non-committal

The Spiritual Law of Pairing

approach, they are laden with conditional requirements, hidden compromises, and endless excuses.

While hiding behind a veneer of Christianese words, their personal constitution is rife with weakness. Being self-deceived, they tout themselves as mighty in faith. But when the battle gets hot, they are nowhere to be found.

We saw this scenario during the Covid-19 scam. Preachers closed their churches and went into hiding. What happened to their Sunday messages about the covenant of healing in Jesus; or His miracles; or the power of His presence? What happened to their messages on faith, courage, and standing on God's Word? Why did they disband? Why didn't they call for a fast and pray *in* the church? Why were they unwilling to pay the price and stand with the truth?

> **Compromise breeches the force of agreement and hinders power. This is the sword that comes with mispairing.**

"Suffer hardship with me, as a good soldier of Christ Jesus. 4 No soldier in active service entangles himself in the affairs of everyday life, so that he may please the one who enlisted him as a soldier. 5 Also if anyone competes as an athlete, he does not win the prize unless he competes according to the rules." (2 Timothy 2: 3-5)

We see people like Demas, Paul's traveling companion. He deserted Paul and went back to the world. Why was he not motivated by Paul's astounding revelations? Why did he find the world more attracting than the treasures of God?

What was in the heart of Hymenaeus, a man of the Ephesian church that he went astray (2 Timothy 2:18)? Why did he defiantly teach damaging doctrine until he was turned over to Satan?

What was in the hearts of Ananias and Saphira? Both were judged unto death—Christians of the faith! Why did they lie to Him and disrespect His presence in the face of the Holy Spirit's signs, wonders,

The Spiritual Law of Pairing

miracles, and manifest glory? Why did they not have any circumspect comprehension of God's dignity?

Matching strengths provide great power. But the brightness of a flashlight is only as powerful as the weakest battery. A chain is only as strong as the weakest link.

> "Do not be mismatched with unbelievers; for what do righteousness and lawlessness share together, or what does light have in common with darkness?" (2 Corinthians 6:14)

How can oil mix with water? How can light and dark co-exist? How can strength and compromise stand in agreement?

If a Christian woman marries an unbeliever, they have no spiritual union in their marriage. They have no agreement in the Spirit. God does not hear the husband's prayer.

> "We know that God doesn't listen to sinners, but He is ready to hear those who worship Him and do His will." (John 9:31. New Living Translation.)

The unbelieving husband cannot be a priest to his family or lead them in the way of righteousness. His family's pilgrimage in Christ is without him. Furthermore, if the children follow his unbelief, it will affect their salvation.

For there to be optimum agreement, **The Spiritual Law of Pairing** requires equal yoking of unity, intensity, and vision. Any compromise breeches the potential power of agreement and hinders progress. This is the sword that comes with mispairing.

In vivid contrast to mispairing, we also find that **Righteous Pairing** produces continuity and power. Jesus unified His apostles and disciples by giving them His glory. They were bonded in the revelation of who He is.

> "And the glory which You [Heavenly Father] have given to Me, I have given to them, that they may be one, just as We are one." (John 17:22. Square brackets added by author for clarity.)

The Spiritual Law of Pairing

Without hesitation, Paul affirmed the principle of pairing when he praised Timothy in a letter to the Philippians:

> "But I hope in the Lord Jesus to send Timothy to you shortly, so that I also may be encouraged when I learn of your condition. 20 For I have no one else of a <u>kindred spirit</u> who will genuinely be concerned for your welfare." (Philippians 2:19-20. Underline by author for added emphasis.)

Other examples of divine pairing are seen in Moses with Joshua, Elijah with Elisha; David with Johnathan; Apollos with Pricilla and Aquila; Luke with Peter—to name a few.

As previously stated, **The Spiritual Law of Pairing** is incredibly powerful when bonded according to the principles of righteousness. For example, from morning till night, Moses judged various disputes among the Israelites. He was wearing down. Because of long delays the people were not well served. As a result, God told Moses that He would take the Holy Spirit's anointing on him (Moses) and place it upon seventy others, who, in turn, would have the same kind of anointing (divine pairing) in order to judge fairly and righteously.

> "Then I will come down and speak with you there, and I will take of the Spirit who is upon you, and will put Him upon them; and they shall bear the burden of the people with you, so that you will not bear it all alone." (Numbers 11:17)

Divine Relationships

By the influence of proximity of one person in relationship to another, the Lord divinely arranges pairing and imparts anointing. Strong churches are formed in this way. They are divinely paired and share in the mutual bond of agreement that produces alignment and strength. When like-minded people come together, they share this design and there is exponential power. But, it is not without contest.

Satan quickly recognizes people that are joined by divine pairing. He understands the potentials. Recognizing the exponential power that comes from such relationships, he studies each person's character while looking for flaws to work his schemes. This is proven by the following examples found in Scripture:

The Spiritual Law of Pairing

- Demas failed to understand the divine relationship God gave him with Paul and went back to the world (2 Timothy 4:10).

- The rich young ruler failed to understand the divine relationship offered him by Jesus and returned to his temporal riches (Matthew 19:16).

- Hymenaeus failed to understand the divine relationship God gave him with Paul. Instead, he continued preaching heresy until he was turned over to Satan (1 Timothy 1:20).

- Barnabas failed to understand the divine relationship he had with Paul and threw it aside over a dispute (Acts 15:36-41).

- Judas failed to understand the divine honor and relationship God gave to him with Jesus and he betrayed Jesus for money (Matthew 26:15).

- Christians fail to recognize how God places them in a church in order to pair them with anointings and insights. They forsake God's assigned placement and go wherever they please.

A mature Christian recognizes the priceless value of *divine pairing*. Such relationships must be guarded against the enemy's tactics that seek to neutralize and destroy them.

If divine relationships are devalued, minimized, or cast aside, Scripture shows that God does not obligate Himself to replace them. Demas, Hymenaeus, Philetus, Alexander, Diotrephes, Judas, Barnabas, the Rich Young Ruler, and many of the Seventy, to name a few, have no record of being paired again in a divine relationship. Therefore, according to **The Spiritual Law of Advancement,** stewardship is required in all that God gives us.

Even though God appointed Paul and Barnabas as a team, Barnabas abandoned Paul. The powerful potential that Barnabas was to have with Paul never actualized because Satan found a way to divide them. However, John-Mark is mentioned a few times in relationship to Paul and is credited with writing the Gospel of Mark.

The Spiritual Law of Pairing

Satan also understands **The Spiritual Law of Pairing** to accomplish his works. His "sent ones" come dressed in polite religious vestige. Inwardly, they are hunters on the prowl that go from church to church. They enter by smooth words and disarm by sweet pleasantries of agreement. They nestle in, gain credibility, and launch their works of destruction.

> **If divinely paired relationships are cast aside, the Lord does not obligate Himself to replace them.**

> "Many will say to Me on that day, 'Lord, Lord, did we not prophesy in Your name, and in Your name cast out demons, and in Your name perform many miracles?' 23 "And then I will declare to them, 'I never knew you; depart from Me, you who practice lawlessness.'" (Matthew 7:22-23)

Practice lawlessness? But wait! They prophesied in the name of the Lord; they did miracles in the name of the Lord; they cast out demons in the name of the Lord. Nonetheless, they crept into churches under the guise of a false anointing and brought dissension and strife. They are mixed streams, mispaired between carnal motivations and spiritual works—they are agents of iniquity seeking opportunity.

During Jesus' trial, he was hustled from Pilate to Herod and then back to Pilate. In Luke 23:12, Pilate and Herod were bitter enemies until Satan paired their personalities against Jesus.

> "Now Herod and Pilate became friends with one another that very day; for before, they had been enemies with each other."

Satan knows how to align people for his own purposes. He knows how to pair complainers, murmurers, and discontented critical people. One must therefore be sensitive to the Holy Spirit at the very onset of any *potential* "pairing". Look for inconsistencies, variations of character, empty words, patterns of failure, consistent flawed patterns. Test and prove them to see if they are from the Lord, or the spirit of darkness?

Ask yourself if the developing *new* alignment has the signature of God's peace? Does the alignment follow the precepts of God's Word?

The Spiritual Law of Pairing

Are there reoccurring issues? Do they have a history of broken relationships?

If the pairing is from the Lord, the Holy Spirit's peace will be there and all things will be done in righteousness. Again, time and circumstance will test and prove it.

Hymenaeus and Alexander

Hymenaeus and Alexander are examples of satanic pairing. Paul describes their faith in the Ephesian church as being "shipwrecked". They were arrogant, haughty, reckless, and unteachable. Therefore, Paul handed them over to Satan (1 Timothy 1:19-20). The presumption of this means they were in Christ, but because of their unapproachable disposition, their faith was shipwrecked.

Being unsubmitted to Kingdom Authority, they recklessly troubled God's work in the local churches and became agents of division and strife. Because of their heresy, they unsettled the faith of many by teaching false doctrines.

Scripture does not detail their obstinance, but later we see Hymenaeus aligned with a man named Philetus—another false teacher (2 Timothy 2:17).

Here again, we see Satan exploiting **The Spiritual Law of Pairing** by spreading his "doctrines of demons" through likeminded pairing. He worked *inside* the church with Hymenaeus and Alexander, and then again with Hymenaeus and Philetus.

To Have Known Paul

What an extreme honor to have known Paul and sit under his teaching! If it were possible, ministers today would pay thousands of dollars to spend a single week with him. Nonetheless, anyone who paired with Paul soon realized his "intensity". It was not easy to keep pace with him knowing that beatings, imprisonments, and trials that awaited him and his companions in nearly every city he preached.

Paul was intensely driven. But the rewards of anointing that he imparted to others by the Holy Spirit were beyond quantifying. Timothy,

The Spiritual Law of Pairing

Titus, and Silvanus are products of Paul's ministry, not to mention many others.

For a season of time, Demas followed Paul quite closely. Paul mentions him affectionately in the closing of his letters on two occasions, one to Philemon and the other to the Colossians. Evidently, Demas was someone with whom people in the church of Colossae and the family of Philemon were familiar.

> "Epaphras, my fellow prisoner in Christ Jesus, greets you, 24, as do Mark, Aristarchus, Demas, Luke, my fellow workers."
> (Philemon 1:23-24)

> "Luke, the beloved physician, sends you his greetings, and also Demas." (Colossians 4:14)

Having close proximity with Paul (**The Spiritual Law of Pairing**), and drawing from his experience, wisdom, knowledge, insights, and revelation, it would naturally inspire a person. But it was not so with Demas.

> "For Demas, having loved this present world, has deserted me and gone to Thessalonica..." (2 Timothy 4:10)

Of all God's servants, Paul was the greatest revelator of the entire Bible. After all, compared to the other Foundation Apostles, the Lord used him to write two-thirds of the New Testament and to establish profound Kingdom insights for all generations. Yet, for some reason, Demas had no concept of Paul's calling, station of authority, or the magnificence of the Holy Spirit's power working through him. Instead, Demas cast the relationship aside for the gain of worldly pleasures.

Again, why did Demas allow himself to be seduced by this world? Why did he cast aside the Lord's "divine pairing" with Paul and trade it for temporary pleasures? Why did he not comprehend the gift God gave him through Paul?

Learn the lessons from their mistakes! Recognize **The Spiritual Law of Pairing**. Guard the divine relationships God places in your life!

The Spiritual Law of Pairing

Protect them! Maintain them! Serve them! They are directly connected to the destiny God has for you, and they are priceless.

If grumbling and murmuring are percolating in your spirit, beware! These are satanically inspired *offenses,* the twin sisters that cultivate a critical and cynical spirit. Its design is to break the bonds of God's divine pairing by fracturing the relationship and disabling your calling, purpose, and influence.

The Lord's vessels are merely clay in the Potter's hands. We are imperfect, flawed by sin, and yet chosen. Being endowed with His anointing and the power of the Spirit, we must approach one another in love and humbly forebear with one another in view of our personal flaws.

Knowing that there are some truths which are not easy to address, it still requires that we speak the truth in love at all times.

> "Make every effort to keep yourselves united in the Spirit, binding yourselves together with peace." *(Ephesian 4:3)*

Chapter Eleven
The Spiritual Law of Forgiveness

"Then summoning him, his lord said to him, 'You wicked slave, I forgave you all that debt because you pleaded with me. 33 'Should you not also have had mercy on your fellow slave, in the same way that I had mercy on you?' 34 "And his lord, moved with anger, handed him over to the torturers until he should repay all that was owed him. 35 "My heavenly Father will also do the same to you, if each of you does not forgive his brother from your heart." (Matthew 18:32-35)

Our Father's Kingdom is established on two primary tenets: giving and forgiving. Just as God forgives, all citizens of God's Kingdom are required to forgive as well. Therefore, **The Spiritual Law of Forgiveness** requires that people forgive one another.

Violating this one spiritual law binds a person to the multitude of their sins. Consequently, the Kingdom of God is closed to whoever refuses to forgive.

Those holding unforgiveness are just as guilty of moral failure as the person they refuse to forgive. Consequently, from God's point of view, He expects people to forgive one another just as He forgives them of their repeated and multiple sins.

The Spiritual Law of Forgiveness

The Curse of Unforgiveness

The sword's penalty related to unforgiveness manifests in many ways, one of which is in the physical body. Sustained unforgiveness creates stress and bitterness in the soul. The heart of such people grows hard, cynical, suspicious, and angry all of which soon turns into bitterness.

Bitterness is the gangrene stage of unforgiveness. It causes chemical changes in the body resulting in loss of sleep, elevated heart rate, and general fatigue. Added to that, the immune system weakens under stress which makes the body susceptible to disease. For this reason, cancer patients are strongly advised to avoid stress at all costs! Stress wears the body down.

The root of bitterness is unforgiveness. Bitterness, the advanced stage of unforgiveness, devours its host. In the church, it isolates people and causes division.

> "See to it that no one comes short of the grace of God; that no root of bitterness springing up causes trouble, and by it many become defiled." *(Hebrews 12:15)*

The sign of an embittered person is often seen by their focused obsession related to an offense. It runs deep in their soul and spreads to everything in their life. They ruminate and rehearse the issue from every angle but never seem to escape it. They are consumed with the offense. Every conversation takes them back to their anger and unforgiveness.

STORY: A friend of mine who is a psychologist was counseling a patient about their pornography addiction. After many talk-sessions, the psychologist asked his patient if he was willing to try an unconventional approach. Being somewhat desperate, the patient agreed.

The patient harbored bitter unforgiveness toward his mother for divorcing his father. After the subject was discussed, the psychologist led his patient in a prayer of forgiveness. Even though this seemed rather "clinical", it removed a hidden sword that was mysteriously connected to the pornography issue.

The Spiritual Law of Forgiveness

The following week, the patient returned for his scheduled therapy session. He joyfully reported that he was set free from the addiction and had no desire or disposition toward pornography.

★★★

Unforgiveness is a wandering vine that entangles multiple areas of the soul. When we hold the sins of others against them, we create bondage to ourselves and open the door to satanic influences.

There are two comparative verses in the New Testament that speak about forgiveness:

> "For if you forgive others for their transgressions, your Heavenly Father will also forgive you." (Matthew 6:14)

> "But if you do not forgive others, then your Father will not forgive the wrongs you have done." (Matthew 6:15)

The above Scriptures clearly affirm God's position: to the one who forgives, and to the one who refuses to forgive.

What is Forgiveness?

Simply stated, to forgive someone from the heart releases a debt against them. Further, it releases the forgiver, sets them free, unburdens their soul, aligns them with God's Kingdom Authority, and gives them favorable standing with the Lord.

However, the forgiven one (if they are *guilty* of an offense) is not necessarily released from the sword. They are simply released by the one whom they offended. But the victim is set free from the burden of holding unforgiveness.

The sword in the life of the one who committed sin is still a matter between them and the Lord. Consequently, the government of sin remains in their life until they do all that is required, including paying restitution when able to do so.

> "Make friends quickly with your opponent at law while you are with him on the way, so that your opponent may not hand you over to the judge, and the judge to the officer, and you be thrown

The Spiritual Law of Forgiveness

into prison. 26 "Truly I say to you, you will not come out of there until you have paid up the last cent." (Matthew 5:25-26)

In reference to the above Scripture, was Jesus speaking of Rome's judicial procedures, or was He speaking of spiritual principles? Obviously, He was not advocating for the Roman court system. Rather, He was speaking of the spiritual principles required in matters of offenses. The above verse of Scripture describes the opponent as a victim, and the debtor as the perpetrator.

The "judge" is the Lord who empowers His spiritual laws. "Making amends quickly" is to stop the action of the sword before it cuts.

Unforgiveness entangles multiple areas of the soul and suppresses progress. When we refuse to forgive, we create bondage to ourselves.

The "prison" is the sword's penalty. It is binding upon a person until the sword is removed by repentance. And, it remains until every "last penny" is paid, that is, until all things are completed in righteousness.

Granting forgiveness is not based on how you feel. In most cases, one's feeling about the person they forgive do not change. They might not like the person, nor are they required to like them. But, what *is* required is that they forgive them from their heart. When they do, it revokes Satan's license against the one who holds unforgiveness.

Making it Personal

As a victim, the only thing required of you is to forgive. To do this, speak to the Father and tell Him that you forgive the person of the offense. If the Lord further directs you, tell the person they are forgiven of the debt owed to you. In some cases, this releases them from bitter regret and condemnation. I have seen such people breakdown under such loads and turn to the Lord once they have been forgiven by the victim.

Satan invariably uses *angry justifications* to keep you reminded of the offense and excite the emotions related to it. This is where you

The Spiritual Law of Forgiveness

remind the enemy that you have forgiven the offender. Once you have forgiven, you do not need to keep reaffirming your forgiveness. You do, however, need to counteract Satan's ploy by telling Satan that you are free from his condemnation.

Healing and Forgiveness

As God's children endowed with His authority, we are told in Psalm's 91:13 that:

> "You will tread upon the lion and cobra, the young lion and the serpent you will trample down."

Unforgiveness is a sin that is forbidden by God. It comes with a sword that is often seen as sickness.

To have authority over Satan, it requires that you walk according to God's righteousness by the wisdom of His spiritual laws. If you violate His Kingdom laws, you create open-door opportunities for Satan. As such, holding unforgiveness against anyone is strictly forbidden by God. It is a serious violation that comes with a sword. Consequently, unforgiveness kicks through a protective wall. By this, the serpent is released to devour. Therefore, stay protected under God's canopy by obedience to His spiritual laws.

The sword afflicts in various ways. It is silent, devouring, and sometimes difficult to comprehend in the "cause-and-effect". It manifests in such things such as addictions, sicknesses, stress, financial loss, broken relationships, accidents, disaster, mishaps, and so forth.

Taking Communion

There are severe warnings about unforgiveness while participating in the Celebration of the Lord's Body and Blood.

> "For he who eats and drinks, eats and drinks judgment to himself if he does not judge the body [Christian relationships] rightly. 30 For this reason many among you are weak and sick and a

The Spiritual Law of Forgiveness

number sleep [have died].*"* (1 Corinthians *11:29-30. Square brackets added by author for clarity.)*

The Spiritual Law of Forgiveness directly intersects with the Holy Communion. Holding unforgiveness while taking communion results in sickness and death! After all, the communion celebrates the forgiveness of sins, salvation, and the healing of our body. If one receives communion while refusing to forgive, it is hypocrisy against the Body and Blood of Jesus.

Confession and Healing

Scripture tells us about healing when we confess our faults one to another. At the same time, Matthew 5:23 tells us that God refuses our gift that is offered to Him until we have done what is required.

> *"Therefore, confess your sins to one another, and pray for one another so that you might be healed. The effective and fervent prayer of a righteous man can accomplish much."(James 5:16)*

> *"So if you are presenting your offering at the altar, and while there you remember that your brother has something* [such as a grievance or legitimate complaint] *against you, 24 leave your offering there at the altar and go. First make peace with your brother, and then come and present your offering." (Matthew 5:23-24. Square brackets added by author for clarity.)*

But what about the people Paul turned over to Satan for the destruction of their flesh? Did he not forgive them?

It is implied in Scripture that he did for one man. Three others, however, refused to repent and were handed over to Satan.

> *"If you forgive the sins of any [by the Holy Spirit's leading], their sins have been forgiven them; if you retain the sins of any [by the Holy Spirit's leading], they have been retained." (John 20:23. Square brackets added by author for clarity.)*

In the above verse, those who refuse to repent, such as those whom Paul turned over to Satan, are judged. Unless they repent, the sword remains active in their lives and cannot be removed. Furthermore,

The Spiritual Law of Forgiveness

under divine authority of the Holy Spirit, the sword is retained against them. We see this example when Peter declared the death of Saphira. The sword came against her immediately after she lied to the Holy Spirit. In yet another instance, Paul declared blindness over Elymas the Sorcerer for interfering with a man's salvation (Acts 13:8-10).

He who forgives, frees himself, but forgiving the offender does not remove the sword from the offender. Only the offender can remove the sword by taking the issue before the Father and asking for forgiveness. After that, the offender must go to the victim, ask for forgiveness (Matthew 5:23), and then offer restitution if he is able.

Chapter Twelve
The Spiritual Law of Advancement

"Then Daniel began distinguishing himself among the commissioners and satraps because he possessed an extraordinary spirit, and the king planned to appoint him over the entire kingdom." **(Daniel 6:3)**

The Spiritual Law of Advancement works in combination with humility, righteousness, faithfulness, and endurance. These four qualities work simultaneously in union one with the other and produce unstoppable results.

Humility

Humility, the opposite of pride, is the gateway into all things of God's Kingdom. It is this virtue that enables repentance and enlarges one's capacity to receive knowledge.

> *"But to this one I will look, to him who is HUMBLE and contrite of spirit, and who trembles at my Word." (Isaiah 66:2)*

> *"Now Moses was very HUMBLE, more than any man who was on the face of the earth." (Numbers 12:3)*

> *"Therefore HUMBLE yourselves under the mighty hand of God that He may exalt you in the proper time." (1 Peter 5:6)*

> *"HUMBLE yourselves in the presence of the Lord, and He will exalt you." (James 4:10)*

The Spiritual Law of Advancement

"He has brought down rulers from their throne and exalted those who were HUMBLE." (Luke 1:52)

"Truly I say you, unless you are converted and become like children, you will not enter the Kingdom of God." (Matthew 18:3)

Pride works in direct opposition to humility. A prideful person cannot be trusted with God's anointing that produces power. After all, it was pride that toppled Satan from his exalted position. And because of pride, God removed King Saul from ruling over Israel. Furthermore, it was pride that blinded the Jewish leaders from seeing Jesus as their Messiah. It is pride that holds an offense. And it is pride that blocks God's blessings.

Humility is the opposite of pride. It is the gateway into God's Kingdom for all things.

To the prideful self-exalting one, God will not entrust him or her with His true riches.

"Pride comes before destruction, and an arrogant spirit before a fall." (Proverbs 16:18)

Righteousness

There are two aspects of righteousness: First, being in Jesus Christ we are the Righteous of the Lord, not by works, but by the finished work of Jesus on the cross. All who are in Jesus are therefore righteous.

The second aspect is our walk. A person that walks righteously, walks with a present-tense awareness of their words and actions. They give careful consideration to God's Word in all that they do. These are the ones who are blessed.

"No good thing will God withhold from those who walk uprightly." (Psalm 84:11b)

Our righteous *position* in Christ says that we are seated with Him in heavenly places (Ephesians 2:6). On this side of Heaven, even though we strive for righteousness, our daily walk is less than our righteous

The Spiritual Law of Advancement

position in Jesus. We must, therefore, be mindful of the Lord's Word so that our condition steadily moves toward our position.

Everyone in Jesus is positionally righteous, but not everyone in Jesus walks consciously righteous. Paul referred to those who walk after the leading of their flesh as carnal, fleshly, babes in Christ. They are soul-driven Christians, not Spirit-led.

> **The anointing God gives is the most dangerous gift of all. It requires true humility and a new wineskin.**

Advancement comes to those who are "Spirit-led", not "soul-driven". The source and working of pride launches from our unregenerated soul. In contrast, the fruits of the Holy Spirit reside in our fully redeemed spirit. For this reason, we must be led by the Holy Spirit through our spirit and not be soul-driven which is often antagonistic toward the Holy Spirit's leading.

The anointing God gives a person is the most dangerous gift of all. It requires true humility with a new wineskin to honorably walk in His anointing and righteousness.

Before God gives His anointing and power, He first considers a person's depth of humility and their walk in righteousness. Those who fear the Lord and tremble at His Word are the candidates He entrusts with great power.

> "The reward of humility and the fear of the Lord are riches, honor, and life." (Proverbs 22:4)

Faithfulness

A faithful steward is one who *carefully* manages and guards the things entrusted to him. There are two primary Scriptures that address **The Spiritual Law of Faithfulness**. First, a person must be proven and tested in those things entrusted to him that are *not* his (1 Timothy 3:10).

The Spiritual Law of Advancement

We are told by the Lord not to despise the day of small beginnings (Zechariah 4:10). This is because the Lord proves and tests a servant by the *faithful stewardship* of that which is another's before he grants the candidate his own. He assigns them small tasks to prove their faithfulness before He gives them large tasks.

> "And if you have not been faithful in the use of that which is another's, who will give you that which is your own?" (Luke 16:12)

A candidate for advancement is eager to serve. They are *detail-minded* in their tasks. They walk with the spirit of excellence as unto the Lord, not just for the approval of men, but doing the will of God from the heart (Ephesian 5:5-7).

Faithfulness is not proven when a person enjoys what they do. It is proven by steadfastness in the excellence of quality when it is something they DO NOT enjoy doing.

Faithful people avoid compromise and presumption in their walk. They have a higher standard of accountability in everything, and they are principle-based in their habits. This is precisely the credo of champions. They see the importance of detail, faithfulness, commitment, endurance, and routine.

A candidate for advancement is eager to serve. He is *detail-minded* and walks in the spirit of excellence in all he does.

Champions value the 1% factor of detailed consistency and faithfulness. Every increment, every detail, every step is important. They value 1% gains and carefully guard against 1% compromises.

James Clear, in his book entitled, <u>Atomic Habits,</u> makes an insightful statement about *habits* which I call, *seeds of manifold strength*.

The Spiritual Law of Advancement

Clear says, "Habits are the compound interest of self-improvement. The same way that money multiplies through compound interest, the [corporate] effects of your habits multiply as you repeat them."[15]

Here again, we see the power of the seed, **The Spiritual Laws of Sowing and Reaping,** and **The Spiritual Law of Pairing.** Mixed seed compromises the result. Mixed seed is composed of counterproductive habits, compromise, inconsistency, excuse-driven delays, and a failure to grasp detail. All of this is weaved between righteous living and besetting sins. It is a composite integrated with virtue and vice. The end result yields, at best, average results. For that reason, repentance and carefully monitoring one's thoughts, words, and deeds is mandatory in overcoming all levels of defeat in order to achieve the maximum blessed life. Consequently, failure to understand **The Spiritual Laws of Sowing and Reaping,** and **The Spiritual Law of Pairing** produces little more than hit and miss blessing.

Joshua the Son of Nun

Joshua was Moses' servant. With all humility, he was faithful to Moses and served him as unto the Lord. It was Joshua that Moses took into the wilderness when the Lord spoke to Moses on the mountain (Exodus 24:13). When the Lord came down and spoke to Moses face-to-face in the *Tent of Meeting*, it was Joshua who stayed behind and worshipped God (Exodus 33:11). Among the twelve spies, only Joshua and Caleb gave an encouraging faith-filled favorable report. The other ten spies spoke fear into everyone (Numbers 13:33). And it was Joshua whom the Lord selected to take Moses' place—after forty years of faithful service to the Lord.

Joshua possessed all the virtues required in **The Spiritual Law of Advancement**: humility, righteousness, faithfulness, and endurance. We see the same virtues in Paul, Timothy, Titus, and hosts of others in the Bible.

---

[15] Clear, James. Atomic Habits, page 16, Penguin Random House, New York, New York 2018

The Spiritual Law of Advancement

※
Consistent and relentless endurance qualifies you for the next promotion. Anyone can start the race, but only the winners finish. The Lord is not looking for "start, stop, and start" sprinters.
※

Endurance

Endurance, patience and perseverance. These words are sometimes used interchangeably, but in reality, they are virtues that produce the same outcome.

For many, this is where the line cuts between victory and nominalism. For lack of endurance, many people give up just before the breakthrough.

When it seems delay has no end in sight, endure! Stay faithful!

When trials or tribulations strike, endure! Stay faithful!

When it seems like everyone has abandoned you, endure! Stay faithful!

In some Bible translations, endurance is used interchangeably with the word *patience*. Regardless of which word is used, it means to persevere while under pain.

Practicing endurance both prove and qualify you for the next promotion. Anyone can start the race, but only the winners finish. This is one reason why many are called but few are chosen (Matthew 22:14). The Lord is not looking for *spurting start and stop* sprinters in the Kingdom. He wants long-distance runners that do not compromise their determination when the winds blow against them in an uphill trudge.

STORY: There was a woman who lived in Darby, Montana. She was a nurse that worked at the hospital in Hamilton nearly twenty miles north along highway 93.

The Spiritual Law of Advancement

Her husband divorced her, left his family including the kids, took the car and money, and ran off with another woman. Unfortunately, all the credit accounts were in her husband's name and she had no personal credit of her own.

Each day, she got out of bed at 2:00 a.m., *walked* twenty miles to the hospital; walked all day during her rounds; and then walked home. Some days she would get a ride, but many days she walked all the way. Because she lived in the opposite direction of her co-workers, no one offered to help with her transportation needs.

Throughout the entire summer, she lost over eighty pounds, trimmed up rather nicely, went through four pairs of shoes, and admirably maintained her job against all adversity.

Ultimately, someone heard of her demise and gave her a good running vehicle.

Her reward came, however, after a great deal of endurance. While enduring, she regained a healthy and youthful look. Her ex-husband was astonished at her transformation and tried to make amends. She showed no interest in him, but, in fact, ended up marrying a handsome and very successful doctor that she worked with at the hospital.

★★★

The life of Paul exemplifies the model of faithfulness and endurance. He began his Gospel ministry around the age of thirty and relentlessly carried it for another thirty-eight years against every opposition and tribulation. Despite his advancing age, nothing stopped him.

> "*Five times I received from the Jews thirty-nine lashes. 25 Three times I was beaten with rods, once I was stoned* [killed and resurrected on the same day], *three times I was shipwrecked, a night and a day I have spent in the deep. 26 I have been on frequent journeys, in dangers from rivers, dangers from robbers, dangers from my countrymen, dangers from the Gentiles, dangers in the city, dangers in the wilderness, dangers on the sea, dangers among false brethren; 27 I have been in labor and hardship, through many sleepless nights, in hunger and thirst, often without food, in cold and exposure. 28 Apart from such external things, there is the daily pressure on me of concern for all the*

The Spiritual Law of Advancement

churches. 29 Who is weak without my being weak? Who is led into sin without my intense concern?" (2 Corinthians 11:24-29)

Endurance is a quality that bears great rewards. This is especially true when we are doing the will of God.

STORY: David Akugo is a dear Christian friend of mine that lives in northern Ghana where the Christian population is one-half of 1% of the people. Muslims form the majority of 98% while the remaining 1.5% are pagans. David's Christian influence, however, is steadily growing through men of great endurance that are righteously paired with him.

One such man walks twelve miles from a remote village to David's headquarters. There, he sits for most of the day listening to a small electronic box called a "Proclaimer". The box measures eight inches long, three inches high, and two inches wide. It has an electronic chip encoded with the *Hausa* language—the primary language of the people in that region. The Proclaimer has three options for power: a 220 volts plug in; a solar panel that charges the batteries; and a hand crank that when turned for about ten minutes yields nearly thirty minutes of playtime.

Sitting in front of the Proclaimer, he listens for hours upon hours where he sets to memory what he hears in the Gospel. He cannot read or write, nor can anyone in his village where there is no electricity. After nearly a full day of listening and memorizing, he walks another twelve miles back to his village where the people are waiting to hear him recite the Gospel. His entire village has been converted to Jesus. He is the voice of the Gospel to them.

Five days a week he does this walking one hundred twenty miles a week to hear and recite the Gospel!

Visiting missionaries bought him a Proclaimer so that he and others can set the entire Gospel to memory. Daily, the villagers meet in the evening to listen. They set the Proclaimer on a rock and gather around to listen to the message.

The Spiritual Law of Advancement

There are no Bibles, commentaries, dictionaries, or other book resources. Everyone memorizes God's spoken words. Their hearts overflow as each one listens to the same source. The purity of the Gospel in their village is remarkable. Moreover, the Holy Spirit visits them with understanding and extraordinary answers to their prayers.

★★★

Endurance is a requisite quality that bears great rewards. This is especially true when doing God's will. The presumption of many Christians, however, is that things get easier when we are in God's will. Surprisingly, it is the exact opposite. Any effective endeavor coming from God Kingdom quickly draws Satan's attention. We are told in Matthew 11:12 that we are at war:

> *"From the days of John the Baptist until now, the Kingdom of Heaven suffers violence and the violent take it by force."* (Matthew 11:12)

War honors no holiday. Do soldiers leave the battle for holiday vacations? In the same way, the work of the Gospel is a declaration of war against the darkness that requires endurance in every aspect.

> *"Therefore, do not throw away your confidence which has great reward. 36 For you have need of endurance so that when you have done the will of God you may receive what was promised."* (Hebrews 11:35-36)

We are again reminded by Scripture that endurance comes with a promise:

> *"Let us not lose heart in doing good, for in due time we will reap if we don't grow weary."* (Galatians 6:9)

In the four virtues contained within **The Spiritual Law of Advancement**: humility, righteousness, faithfulness, and endurance, each one must be carefully considered. Defeat is guaranteed by compromising any one of the four. All four virtues work in concert together. It is important, therefore, that every detail is considered in **The Spiritual Law of Advancement**.

The Spiritual Law of Advancement

> *War honors no holiday. What type of soldier leaves the battle to go on vacation? The Gospel is a declaration of war that requires endurance in every aspect.*

If a person is humble but unfaithful, his humility does not compensate for the difference. If he is righteous but has no endurance, his integrity cannot compensate for the difference.

The four virtues are like legs on a table. Stability is achieved when all four legs are equal length.

Are they are part of your life's constitution? If not, develop them. Increase in them. Be strong in them. In so doing, spiritual advancement is the natural outcome.

> *"For the eyes of the Lord move to and fro throughout the earth that He may strongly support those whose heart is completely His." (2 Chronicles 16:9)*

Chapter Thirteen
God's 100% Commitment to You

"Bless the LORD, O my soul, and all that is within me, bless His holy name. 2 Bless the LORD, O my soul, and forget none of His benefits; 3 who pardons all your iniquities, who heals all your diseases; 4 who redeems your life from the pit, who crowns you with lovingkindness and compassion, 5 who satisfies your years with good things, so that your youth is renewed like the eagle." (Psalm 103:1-5)

Our compassionate Heavenly Father wants us to have the fulness of life, not only in the eternity to come, but on this side of Heaven as well. For this reason, Jesus provided all the means for life and peace in this present life. Therefore, let us minimize nothing of His death and suffering. Instead, let us avail ourselves to all He has for us!

During the span of one's earthly life, mistakes are numerous. Most of the time, we have no idea why things exist as they do, or how they evolved into what they became. Nonetheless, a great portion of our problems are the decisions we make or have made through violations of God's spiritual laws.

For example, promiscuity, addictions, and self-affliction are often the consequences of molested children that grow up with broken souls.

Curses decreed over a child by parents often set the destiny of a child's life.

God's 100% Commitment to You

The Spiritual Law of the Seed says that all things produce after their kind. Wayward parents living in cycles of defeat pass their sword onto their children, and the children become like their parents who then pass the sword onto their children. The cycle of generational curses continue and no one knows why.

While all may seem dismal and hopeless, the answer lies in the hands of the Lord. There is a solution! He knows the cause and He knows the answer.

Starting from the fall of Adam, every person is born with a fallen nature. For this reason, you need to be born again through Jesus Christ in order to break the cycles and patterns of destruction. This is the starting point.

If you are like many Christians, mostly likely you were ignorant of God's spiritual laws while you were stacking up the penalties—plenty of them. Consequently, there may be multiple swords in your life.

Some people have more swords than a porcupine has quills. However, there is good news! When you come to Christ (if you haven't already) the old self has passed away, new potentials come into play, and new things are launched into motion. The swords are falling off.

Salvation gives you *sonship* with your Heavenly Father! From this privileged position in life, the cleanup process by God's Word commences. The Holy Spirit begins the process of leading you out of the swamp.

> "Therefore, if anyone is in Christ, he is a new creature; the old things have passed away; behold new things have come."
> (2 Corinthian 5:17)

Cleaning Up

In the process of change, three key Scriptures apply to the context of such challenge:

> "For I am confident of this very thing, that He who began a good work in you will perfect it until the day of Jesus Christ." *(Philippians 1:6)*

God's 100% Commitment to You

"I am the Vine; you are the branches. The one who remains in Me and I in him bears much fruit, for [otherwise] *apart from Me* [that is, cut off from vital union with Me] *you can do nothing.'"*
(John 15:5. The Amplified Bible)

"If you abide in Me, and My words abide in you, ask whatever you wish, and it will be done for you. 8 "My Father is glorified by this, that you bear much fruit, and so prove to be My disciples.'"
(John 15:7-8)

Keep in mind, you did not start your salvation, and you cannot finish yourself. The beginning, the process, and the end exclusively belong to the work of Jesus. While you were still in your sins and spiritually dead, Jesus came to you and gave you truth. Your obligation is to submitt to His leading; keep His Word in your heart; humbly obey Him; and let Him do the work.

> **It is imperative to remember that you did not start yourself in Christ and you cannot finish yourself in Christ. Only Jesus can finish you.**

Apart from Him, you can do nothing. Every success in life comes through Him by obedience to His spiritual laws.

Painfully, the Father's pruning process makes you stronger in Jesus. He does the pruning, not you, and not the rules of religion. You must look to Him for all things while going forward. He knows what to do. He is the skilled surgeon whose diagnostic accuracy is 100%. And...He never fails.

But if all things are new, exactly *what* is new? After all, you continue to age; you are still tempted; you still have old mindsets and habits...so what things have become new?

There are three parts to every person: the spirit, soul, and body. When you are born again, the only part that is saved is your spirit. At the moment of salvation, your Heavenly Father gave you a resident measure of faith so that you can believe everything about Him. This measure of faith is sufficient to believe God for everything in your life

God's 100% Commitment to You

and everything He tells you. In contrast, before He gave you faith to believe (Ephesians 2:8 ; Romans 12:3), nothing or very little of Him and His Kingdom made any sense to you.

While your spirit is saved, your mind is in the *process* of being saved. The renewal process starts at the moment of salvation (Ephesians 4:22-23). Thus, when you sin, you sin from that part of your unregenerated soul, the old self, the unrenewed part yet to be submitted to Jesus (see Romans 7).

When you are born again, God gives you a new nature through your spirit. But...because you have free moral will, you can choose to follow the dictates of your old unregenerated soul and submit to the lusts of the world that you formerly knew. With that being true, you quickly discover a dilemma. There is a conflict between the new nature you possess in your spirit through Jesus and the dictates that flow from that part of your unregenerated soul.

The *renewed* part of your mind is no longer contrary to the Word of God. At the same time, your spirit is fully receptive to whatever the Lord tells you. For this reason, you must be *Spirit-led*, not soul-led. You must be sensitive to the Holy Spirit and follow His leading as He speaks to your spirit—His Spirit to your spirit.

> *"For the mind set on the flesh is death, but the mind set on the Spirit is life and peace, 8 because the mind set on the flesh is hostile toward God; for it does not subject itself to the law of God; for it is not even able to do so."* (Romans 8:7-8)

> *"If indeed you have heard Him and have been taught in Him, just as truth is in Jesus, 22 that, in reference to your former manner of life, you lay aside the old self, which is being corrupted in accordance with the lusts of deceit, 23 and that you be renewed in the spirt of your mind, 24 and put on the new self which is in the likeness of God created in righteousness and holiness of the truth."* (Ephesians 4:21-24)

Finally, your physical body will be transformed at the time of the rapture and you will receive a glorified, ageless, perfect body.

God's 100% Commitment to You

From the instant you are saved, you have solutions to every sword in your present life—but only through Jesus Christ.

You have a new spiritual identification in Jesus Christ. You are equipped for war to fight *in* the victory that Jesus already won for you.

Because Jesus defeated Satan, Satan has no power over you except what you give him through lust. Once you choose to fight against the temptations of Satan, victory is already decided if you follow the Holy Spirit.

The Sword Must Go

The Father desires victory for you in every area of your life. The swords came from the old habits, thoughts, and patterns. And, there are penalties associated with them.

To remove the sword, the first thing you must do is pray. The Lord will then do one of three things or in combination: (1) He will change the circumstance. (2) He will change *you* in the circumstance. (3) He will change you *and* the circumstance.

Keep in mind that from the point of your salvation forward, you have solutions to every sword in life.

Something will change. The sword will be removed. If you seek the Lord and follow His Spirit, every sword will be removed.

Every Great Leader

Every great leader in the Bible had failures, triumphs, and swords. But, they overcame by the power of the Lord and moved forward. So will you, if you refuse to accept defeat.

The most difficult people to help are those who adjust their lifestyles to compatibly live with the enemy's affliction. They surrender to defeat. They accept their sickness and then design their life around it. Yet, God promises to give them total victory...if they will fight.

God's 100% Commitment to You

STORY: A middle-aged woman in the city where I was a policeman acquired polio when she was a teenager. Everything in her house was remodeled to the height of her wheelchair.

She would have episodic bouts of loneliness and often called the police department for the most ridiculous issues. In truth, it was a ploy for someone to visit with her.

The dispatchers understood her tactics. Accordingly, the department had a strategy to help the officers politely escape her insistence for them to sit and have tea with her. Ten minutes or so after the officer arrived, the dispatcher radioed the officer and sent him to another call. The call was then broadcast on his portable radio for her to hear.

On one occasion, I asked the lady if she would like to be healed. Her response came without hesitation. She told me she was happy with the life she had known for thirty years.

Knowing the Lord's healing power which I have seen on many occasions when I prayed for people in Africa, it was difficult for me to envision a life that surrendered to such limitation.

★★★

Never surrender to Satan. You need to fight for total victory. Never yield an inch of ground to him. You must guard against accommodating him in any degree.

Listen to your speech. Listen to your words. Do they claim ownership of your sickness, circumstance, and situation? Do they agree with defeat? Sometimes we say things that empower and license the enemy. "I have cancer." "I hate my life." "I can't keep going on this way."

These are all claims of ownership. Such claims need to be denounced. You did not ask for sickness, disease, defeat, or anything from Satan. Those were things he sent against you. Therefore, change your speech and stop giving place to them by claiming ownership of them.

> *"Grace and peace be multiplied to you in the knowledge of God and of Jesus our Lord; seeing that His divine power has granted to us everything pertaining to life and godliness, through the true*

God's 100% Commitment to You

knowledge of Him who called us by His own glory and excellence." (2 Peter 1:3)

Famous Swords

Adam failed to rescue Eve after she sinned. Instead, he joined her in the same sin.

Abraham surrendered his wife on two different occasions when kings wanted to take her into their harem and have sex with her. God, however, delivered Sarah.

Moses murdered an Egyptian soldier who struck one of the Hebrew slaves. Moses then fled to the desert.

David committed adultery with Bathsheba, killed her husband, a righteous man, then married her even though she was a Gentile woman.

The Foundational Apostles abandoned Jesus during His greatest trial.

The Apostle Paul persecuted the early church and consented to the death of Stephen and other Christians.

Sampson fell into the arms of a seducing woman and lost his power.

They all had swords in their lives. But, the Lord delivered them and the swords were removed.

Again, start with prayer. Fasting is sometimes required when something needs revealed by the Holy Spirit. David did this to find out why there was famine was in the land.

Repentance is the power of obedience that revokes the license of the enemy.

Through prayer, you receive direction. In God's Written Word, you will discover which spiritual law(s) apply to the sword in question. It is here you must apply God's Word and use your spiritual weapons:

God's 100% Commitment to You

"For those we walk in the flesh, we do not war according to the flesh. 4 For the weapons of our warfare are not carnal but mighty in God for pulling down strongholds, 5 casting down arguments and every high thing that exalts itself against the knowledge of God, bringing every thought into captivity to the obedience of Christ 6 and being ready to punish all disobedience when your obedience is fulfilled." (2 Corinthians 10:3-6)

What are your weapons? Prayer, faith, praise, worship, thanksgiving, your authority in Christ to bind and loosen, repentance, and forgiveness. You have authority in Christ. By His Word, the sword is removed once the requirements of His Word are completed. This is why the Scripture says, *"And being ready to punish all disobedience when your obedience is fulfilled."*

Repentance is a weapon that revokes the enemy's license.

Forgiving others removes your sins held against you. (Mark 4:25-26)

In prayer, God reveals where the sword has license and what you must do to remove it. Much of this is covered in Chapter Five.

The Hard Cases

Some cases are more complicated than others. And to be frank about it, even though the sin is forgiven and the sword is removed, the government of the sin remains:

- People marry the wrong people, have children, then divorce. The divorce leaves a wake of disaster with broken souls.

- Aborting a child is a forgivable sin, but the memory remains.

- A young man sitting in prison is forgiven and the sword is removed, but years of his life were spent sitting in a cell.

- A driver with no criminal record unintentionally killed someone in a vehicle accident. He is forgiven of manslaughter but spends twenty-years in prison.

God's 100% Commitment to You

- A single act produces a lifetime of regret, and nothing can change the outcome.

> *Many of God's leaders had swords in their lives. But, the Lord delivered them and the swords were removed.*

Even though repentance removes the sword, what if the damages are not reversable, such as the death of a person, or costs beyond your ability to pay? Does this mean the sword remains *if* you have not done what is required *according to your ability*, the short answer is yes.

The characteristics of the sword and the government of sin may seem like one and the same, but they are not. The sword limits our lives in specific areas until it is removed. Once the sword is removed, you are free to move forward without its limitations. The government of our sin, however, may continue to shadow us.

Some labels are never forgotten. King David, for example, was forgiven of his sins, but his record is memorized forever.

He will again rule over Israel during the 1000-Year Reign of the Lord Jesus. David's throne will be directly under the throne of the Lord, and Israel will be the capital of the world!

> *The characteristics of the sword and the government of sin may seem as one and the same, but they are different.*

Referring again to the three actions where God changes the circumstance, changes the person, or changes the circumstance and the person, God gives grace through it all.

If the circumstance is unchangeable and the government of sin is permanently inscribed upon your life, God will change you *in the circumstance*.

God's 100% Commitment to You

EXAMPLE: Joseph could not change his circumstance when he was sold as a slave to Potiphar's house. Instead, God gave him grace and favor with Potiphar (Genesis 39:1-33).

When Potiphar's wife falsely accused Joseph of trying to rape her, he was sent to prison but God was with him. In prison, God prospered Joseph. Through his position as a trustee, he prophetically interpreted a dream to an important person of Pharoah's court. Eventually, Joseph was recommended to stand before Pharoah and prophetically interpret Pharoah's dream. Joseph found favor with Pharoah who made him second in charge of Egypt. It was God directing, creating, composing, and making everything work for Joseph's benefit whom He would use to save all of Israel.

Throughout Joseph's trials and tribulations, he remained righteous and waited for the Lord. Eventually, in due time, God changed the circumstance.

Hope is a powerful force when waiting on the Lord. Hope sustains you and gives you confidence in God's faithfulness who works all things to your benefit. You have hope because you know He loves you.

If your focus is always on the past, regret will embitter your soul. Faith looks forward, not back. It looks to the goodness of God. God's faithfulness makes all things work together, and His grace sustains you until the solution comes.

> *"And we know that God causes all things to work together for good to those who love God, to those who are called according to His purpose."* (Romans 8:28)

Impatiently, Sarah wanted the promised son. She looked at things naturally instead of spiritually and decided to take control. She told Abraham to go into her maid, Hagar, an Egyptian woman, and raise up a son for her instead of waiting on the Lord. (In Abraham's era, this was a custom of the land.)

Hagar conceived and brought forth a son named Ishmael. Ishmael became the Father of twelve tribes racially known as the "Arabs" of

God's 100% Commitment to You

which the Islamic world is largely comprised. By their genetic code, Arabs are half Egyptian and half Jewish.

Precisely true to the prophecy given Hagar concerning Ishmael, his descendants are a problematic people:

> *"I* [the Lord] *will greatly multiply your offspring so that they will be too numerous to count. 11 The Angel of the Lord* [who is Jesus Christ], *proceeded. 'Behold, you have conceived and will bear a son. And you shall name him Ishmael, for the Lord the heard your cry of affliction. 12 He will be a wild donkey of a man and his hand will be against everyone, and everyone's hand will be against him, and he will live in hostility toward all his brothers.'"*
> (Genesis 16:10-12. Square brackets added by author for clarity.)

While waiting for the Lord, do not tell Him how or when to do anything. Abraham and Sarah discovered this very principle. Through her impatience and unbelief, their personal self-serving decision is now a global disaster. Today, we have the Arab and Israeli conflict, a conflict that in our near future, will lead to WWIII.

Let Nothing Stop You

Identify the sword through prayer. By repentance, remove it with confession and be forgiven. (The entire subject of repentance, as previously stated, is covered in Chapter Five.)

After the sword is removed, stop the regrets. Turn to the Lord concerning the government of your sin. He will grant you both wisdom and favor in dealing with the aftermath of sin. The Lord will prosper you and make everything work together for your good.

> *"Forgetting those things which are behind and reaching forward to those things which are ahead, I press on toward the goal for the prize of the upward call of God in Christ Jesus."*
> (Philippians 3:13-14)

Be well and be wise!

Made in the USA
Middletown, DE
27 July 2024